Math Projects

Author: Joyce A. Stulgis-Blalock

Illustrator: Ron Blalock

Editors: Mary Dieterich and Sarah M. Anderson

Proofreader: Margaret Brown

COPYRIGHT © 2011 Mark Twain Media, Inc.

ISBN 978-1-58037-575-7

Printing No. CD-404155

Mark Twain Media, Inc., Publishers
Distributed by Carson-Dellosa Publishing LLC

Visit us at www.carsondellosa.com

Standards reprinted with permission from *Principles and Standards for School Mathematics*, copyright 2000 by the National Council of Teachers of Mathematics. All rights reserved. No endorsement by NCTM is implied.

TABLE OF CONTENTS

e = easy
a = average
c = challenging

AN INTRODUCTION TO THE *MATH PROJECTS* BOOK

How to use this book:

1. According to the needs of the students, the teacher chooses a project based on the NCTM Math Standard(s) found on the Teacher Notes Pages.
2. The teacher makes a choice of the project that would teach and/or reinforce the Standard or concept.
3. Direct instruction is given by the instructor for three or four days, followed by practice work to evaluate student understanding.
4. He/she makes copies of the chosen project page, one per student.
5. The teacher gathers the materials needed, listed on the Teacher Notes Pages.
6. The pages and materials are distributed to students.
7. The assignments are read carefully WITH the students.
8. As students work, the instructor helps individuals, evaluates the task at hand, or has small-group instruction.
9. As students complete the project, they do enrichment material.
10. For special education students or learning-challenged students, part of a project may be assigned.

How this book can help your students:

1. It provides students with challenging mathematics projects that reinforce the NCTM Mathematics Standards and reinforce basic skills.
2. The book provides real-life application of math in daily life.
3. It enables students to experience a variety of ways to complete a project, for example, with a partner, a small group, or alone.
4. It provides students with interesting hands-on activities that promote creative problem solving.
5. This book can be used with or without your math curriculum.

How this book can help you, the teacher:

1. Teachers have a complete one-week or two-week lesson plan. Simply staple a project page into the plan book.
2. The projects are student-directed, needing very little explanation from the teacher.
3. As students work, the teacher is free to evaluate or conduct small-group instruction.
4. Projects provide many areas that can be evaluated. Each project involves computation, reading, written communication, oral communication skills, social skills, and at times, artistic skills.

TEACHER NOTES FOR *MATH PROJECT* PAGES

Page 1 - A Playground Game Design

Students must know:

- how to find the area of a square, rectangle, circle, and triangle
- how to enlarge a drawing by setting up ratios, ex. 1 cm = 1 meter

NCTM Standard - Geometry analyze properties of two-dimensional geometric shapes; understand relationships among areas of different shapes

Materials needed:
- pencil   • erasers
- loose-leaf paper
- rulers, yardsticks, or meter sticks
- large poster or mural paper

Can be used when students are studying length measurement and just beginning to find the area of a space, such as a rectangle or square.

Page 2 - Algebraic Equations

Students must know:

- how to write simple story problems following a certain pattern, ex. Billy has some cars. Bob has 2 more cars than Billy. Together, they have 8 cars. How many does each have? An equation is: $n + (2 + n) = 8$. (The teacher will have to model several problems before the students will be able to write an equation from a problem.)
- how to solve equations using the inverse operation on both sides of the equation

NCTM Standard - Algebra use symbolic algebra to represent problems; model and solve problems using graphs, tables, and equations

Materials needed:
- pencils
- loose-leaf paper
- 3 large pieces of paper for every pair of students to record final problems
- brightly colored markers

Can be used when students are just beginning to learn how to form an equation with an unknown from a simple story problem.

Page 3 - Analyzing Graphs

Students must know:

- how to read a graph
- how to develop questions about data in a graph
- how to compare graphs showing similar data
- how to write story problems about graph data

NCTM Standard - Data Analysis and Probability select and use appropriate statistical methods to analyze data; use observations about differences between two or more samples to develop conjectures

Materials needed:
- pencils   • loose-leaf paper
- copies of bar graphs, line graphs, or pictographs from newspapers, workbooks, or magazines

Can be used when students need to learn how to look with more depth into graphs.

Page 4 - Bicycle Trip Plan

Students must know:

- how to read a road map using a distance scale
- how to determine the different types of roads on a map
- how to calculate distance vs. time problems

NCTM Standards - Measurement and Problem Solving solve problems involving scale factors, using ratio and proportion; make a table to solve a problem

Materials needed:
- pencils   • loose-leaf paper
- several state, province, or county road maps
- chart paper or poster board

Can be used when students are learning how to read map legends and to determine the miles from one place to another.

Page 5 - Budgeting

Students must know:

- how to draw circles with a compass
- how to convert parts of a monthly income into percent increments
- how to convert percents into degrees within a circle
- how to use a protractor to draw angles within a circle

NCTM Standards - Number and Operations and Geometry compute fluently; work flexibly with percents; select and apply techniques and tools to find angle measurements

Materials needed:
- large chart paper or   • compass
  poster board   • calculators
- protractor   • markers or crayons

Can be used when students are learning how to make a budget, how to determine percentages of each budgeted item, and how to make a circle graph and divide it into degrees to display the budget.

TEACHER NOTES FOR *MATH PROJECT* PAGES (cont.)

Page 6 - Building a Dog Area

Students must know:

- how to find the perimeter and area of various shapes: a square, circle, triangle, rectangle, pentagon, or hexagon, etc.
- how to calculate costs of material: ex. If 1 yard of fence is $8.00, then 12 yards = $96.00.

NCTM Standards - Measurement and Problem Solving understand and use units of measurement to measure area; use formulas to determine area of various shapes; draw a picture to solve a problem

Materials needed:
- newspaper ads and/or catalogs from hardware stores
- large piece of art paper or poster paper
- markers and calculators

Can be used when studying area and finding area of rectangles, squares, circles, and pentagons or hexagons; also how to find the best prices for items in newspaper ads.

Page 7 - Collecting Data

Students must know:

- how to make recording (tally) charts on which to record data
- how to transfer collected data into a bar or line graph
- how to label graphs with title, horizontal axis label, and vertical axis label
- how to orally present information in a graph

NCTM Standard - Data Analysis and Probability formulate questions; design studies; collect data; select, create, and use appropriate graphical representations of data

Materials needed:
- paper for recording charts
- graph paper
- chart paper, poster board, or large graph paper
- all kinds of physical education equipment: balls, jump ropes, etc.

Can be used when just beginning to learn how to collect data from trials of their own design.

Page 8 - Comparing Grass Growth vs. Price

Students must know:

- how to calculate unit price, if price per pound of seed is $1.00, then the price per ounce would be $1.00 ÷ 16 = $0.0625
- how to make a recording chart
- how to develop a graph from the data they collect

NCTM Standards - Data Analysis and Probability and Connections formulate questions; design studies; collect data; select, create, and use appropriate graphical representations of data; apply mathematics in contexts outside of mathematics

Materials needed:
- grass seed, 25 of each type of seed for each pair of students (try to purchase at least 4 types of seed)
- 4 one-gallon plastic milk containers for each pair of students
- potting soil, about 10–20 quarts
- recording chart and graph paper

Can be used when students are learning to determine unit price for one ounce of an item, then to collect data and make a graph showing the fastest-germinating type of grass.

Page 9 - Comparing Prices and Ingredients of Cereals

Students must know:
- how to calculate price per ounce
- how to read a nutrition label
- how to read the pricing labels of various cereals in a grocery store
- how to make a recording chart
- how to develop a graph from the data collected

NCTM Standard - Data Analysis and Probability formulate questions; design studies; collect data; select, create, and use appropriate graphical representations of data

Materials needed:
- various cereal boxes (that students can share)
- price of each cereal per ounce
- recording chart for each pair
- graph paper, large graph paper, or poster board

Can be used when studying nutritional value as opposed to unit price or price per ounce.

Page 10 - Conducting a Metric Olympics

Students must know:

- how to measure length (centimeters, meters)
- how to measure weight (grams, kilograms)
- how to measure capacity (milliliters, liters)
- general metric measurement (this lesson is good as a culmination to a metric unit)
- how to make various kinds of recording charts and how to schedule events

NCTM Standards - Measurement and Data Analysis and Probability understand both metric and customary systems of measurement; collect, organize, and display data

Materials needed:
- index cards for a clear set of directions and to list the rules
- paper for recording charts
- banner paper or computer banner software
- meter sticks, gram scales, gravel, cotton balls, paper clips, 2-L containers, eyedropper, 100-milliliter cups

Can be used when students have completed a unit on metric measurement, length, capacity, and weight.

TEACHER NOTES FOR *MATH PROJECT* PAGES (cont.)

Page 11 - Connecting Decimals and Fractions

Students must know:

- how to calculate fraction-to-decimal equivalents and the reverse, decimals to fractions
- how to write a very clear set of directions
- how to make a connect-the-dots circle as explained on student page 11
- how to make a Concentration game

NCTM Standard - Number and Operations
understand relationships among numbers and work flexibly with fractions and decimals

Materials needed:
- calculators
- white art paper
- lots of small index cards
- pencils, loose-leaf paper, and markers

Can be used when students need reinforcement in thinking of fractions and decimals interchangeably.

Page 12 - Coordinate Puzzles

Students must know:

- how to graph coordinates on a four-quadrant piece of graph paper (positive and negative numbers)
- how to draw a simple, one-continuous-line drawing, and then assign coordinates every so often to enable another student to solve the "connect-the-dots" picture

NCTM Standard - Geometry specify locations using coordinate geometry; use coordinate geometry to examine special geometric shapes

Materials needed:
- lots of 4-quadrant (coordinate) graph paper as shown on the student page
- very large graph paper (if available)
- pencils and fine-point markers

Can be used as reinforcement of graphing coordinates.

Page 13 - Dancing Geometric Shapes

Students must know:

- the meaning of the terms: vertex, vertical and horizontal axis, and coordinates
- the geometric moves: translation, rotation, reflection
- what a 45˚, 90˚,180˚, and a 360˚ degree turn on a particular coordinate point means (this can be modeled on an overhead projector or chalkboard)

NCTM Standard - Geometry describe sizes, positions, and orientations of shapes under informal transformations, such as slide, flip, and turn

Materials needed:
- 1/2 or 1 inch-sized square graph paper for each student
- a piece of 4-quadrant coordinate plane graph paper for each student
- pencils, loose-leaf paper

Can be used as a culminating activity after the students know the geometric moves: translation, reflection, and rotation. They also have to know how to interpret coordinate graphs, for example: where to find (+5,-7) on a four-quadrant graph.

Page 14 - Designing the Perfect Classroom

Students must know:

- what pieces of furniture are an absolute necessity in a classroom
- what the needs of the teacher are, in terms of teaching items and storing items (projectors, chalkboards, etc.)
- what the needs of the students are (students may need to interview each other)
- the technology that is needed
- to include lighting, windows, doors, quick fire-escape routes, etc.

NCTM Standards - Measurement and Connections understand and use units of measurement to measure area; recognize and apply mathematics outside of mathematics

Materials needed:
- many office-supply catalogs from various companies
- loose-leaf paper to brainstorm
- chart paper to record purchases
- (optional) mural paper to draw the classroom or thin cardboard to make a small model

Can be used after the students know how to find the area of a particular floor space, for example: a square space, a rectangular space, a triangular space, and a circular space; also, how to choose classroom furniture and equipment and determine costs of these items.

TEACHER NOTES FOR *MATH PROJECT* PAGES (cont.)

Page 15 - Developing a Summer Business

Students must know:

- how to organize a group to accomplish a large task
- that a successful business has to make a certain percentage profit and how to calculate that percentage
- to decide on a service, an item, or items to sell
- to determine the jobs that need to be filled

NCTM Standard - Number and Operations
understand ways of representing numbers and work flexibly with fractions, decimals, and percents

Materials needed:

- various catalogs with office supplies, small items, candy, etc.
- paper, pencils, and markers
- poster board that has been cut in half lengthwise, one per group

Can be done when students need reinforcement in organizational skills; for example, all the planning needed to undertake a task such as forming a small business; also, basic computation skill reinforcement.

Page 16 - Draw a Diagram to Solve a Problem

Students must know:

- how to calculate all types of fraction problems
- how to write story problems
- how drawing a diagram can help them find a solution to a complicated problem
- how to use graph paper to work out a solution

NCTM Standard - Problem Solving
draw a picture to solve a problem; use graph paper as a tool to come to a solution

Materials needed:

- graph paper
- computer time for each pair of students
- loose-leaf paper and pencils

Solution: Go 3 steps from bottom step, 90° turn to right, go 5 steps. Soda is at your feet.

Can be used to reinforce problem solving by drawing a diagram on graph paper.

Page 17 - Drawing Proportionate Figures

Students must know:

- how to form a ratio and set up proportions
- how to solve for an unknown in a proportion using cross-multiplication, then division, for ex. 1.5/2.8 as 3/n
- how to measure length using a centimeter ruler
- how to write centimeters as decimals

NCTM Standard - Measurement
solve problems involving scale factors, using ratio and proportion

Materials needed:

- centimeter rulers
- large art paper 18" x 24" for each student
- markers and/or crayons
- calculators

Can be used after students have practiced setting up proportions and solving them to find an unknown, for example: 3/5 as 8/n = 5 x 8 = 40, then 40 ÷ 3 = n or 13.33.

Page 18 - Fractional Robots

Students must know:

- how to calculate the area of a square, a rectangle, and a triangle
- how to determine the fractional part one shape is of a large piece of paper, for ex. 1/4 of 400 cm² = 100 cm²
- how to find what percentage one part is of a large piece of paper, for ex. 1/4 of 400 cm² = 100 cm², therefore, 100 cm² = 25% of the whole piece

NCTM Standard - Number and Operations
understand ways of representing numbers and work flexibly with fractions, decimals, and percents

Materials needed:

- one piece of white art paper measuring 20 cm x 20 cm per student
- one piece of white, heavy stock paper measuring 40 cm x 40 cm per student
- one large poster board for each student (any color)
- pencils, crayons, markers, calculators

Can be used when students are learning to see the connection between fractions and percents, for example: 1/2 = 50% and 2/5 = 40%.

Page 19 - Fractional Floor Plans

Students must know:

- how to read a blueprint of a house floor plan
- how to draw a simple house floor plan of their own design
- how to calculate square footage
- how to write and solve fraction story problems
- how to determine fractional parts of a whole or a part ex. What fraction of all the rooms are the bathrooms?

NCTM Standards - Measurement and Problem Solving
understand and use units of measurement to measure area; draw a picture to solve a problem

Materials needed:

- copies of various house floor plans for each pair of students
- square centimeter graph paper
- loose-leaf paper, pencils

Can be used when students are studying square footage and after they have learned addition and subtraction of fractions.

TEACHER NOTES FOR *MATH PROJECT* PAGES (cont.)

Page 20 - Fractionated Fairy Tales

Students must know:

- how to do all calculations involving fractions:
  - addition
  - subtraction
  - multiplication
  - division
- how to write story problems

NCTM Standard - Number and Operations
compute fluently (with fractions) and understand ways of representing numbers; work flexibly with fractions

Materials needed:
- pencils and loose-leaf paper
- several sheets of chart paper for each student
- wide-tip color markers

Can be used after students have learned addition, subtraction, multiplication, and division of fractions and after they know how to solve and write multi-step story problems.

Page 21 - Fraction Card Games

Students must know:

- the basic concepts of fractions:
  - equivalent fractions, simplifying fractions
  - identifying fractions - proper, improper, and mixed
  - greatest common factors
  - least common multiple
  - converting improper fractions to mixed numbers

NCTM Standard - Number and Operations
compute fluently (with fractions) and understand ways of representing numbers; work flexibly with fractions

Materials needed:
- many packages of small index cards
- markers
- paper and pencils

Can be used as the teacher is just introducing fraction basics, for example: equivalent fractions, simplifying fractions, greatest common factors, least common multiples, converting mixed numbers to improper fractions, and the reverse of that.

Page 22 - Fraction Puzzle Booklets

Students must know:

- the basic concepts of fractions:
  - equivalent fractions
  - ordering fractions
  - simplifying fractions
  - changing improper fractions to mixed numbers
  - least common multiple and greatest common factor

NCTM Standard - Number and Operations
compute fluently (with fractions) and understand ways of representing numbers; work flexibly with fractions

Materials needed:
- a package of copier paper
- computer time to type out pages
- markers to print out the puzzles

Can be used after students have learned the basic concepts of fractions as mentioned in page 21 above.

Page 23 - Geometric Rockets

Students must know:

- how to find the area of the following shapes using the formulas given on the student page:
  - square and rectangle
  - triangle
  - circle
  - parallelogram
- the basic structure of a space rocket

NCTM Standards - Geometry and Measurement
understand and use units of measurement to measure area; use formulas to determine area of various shapes

Materials needed:
- art paper measuring 9" x 12" for each student
- rulers, pencils, compasses, and protractors
- poster board or large art paper for each student

Can be used to reinforce finding the area of basic geometric shapes.

Page 24 - Geometry Zip-Around Game

Students must know:

- how to use their math glossary or math book to find definitions of geometry terms (Teacher, you will have to divide the geometry sections of the book into 12 to 15 sections, one section for each pair of students.)
- how to follow the directions very carefully to make a successful zip-around game

NCTM Standard - Geometry
describe, classify, and understand relationships among two- and three-dimensional objects; using defining properties; understand relations between angles, side lengths, perimeters, surface areas, and volumes

Materials needed:
- 10–15 large (5" x 8") index cards for each pair of students
- one geometry section of math book or math resource books

Can be used as students are learning definitions of geometric terms.

TEACHER NOTES FOR *MATH PROJECT* PAGES (cont.)

Page 25 - Geometry Dictionary

Students must know:

• basic geometry terms
• how to explain math terms in simple language for younger students
• how to draw pictures of the geometric shapes they will define

NCTM Standard - Geometry describe, classify, and understand relationships among two- and three-dimensional objects; using defining properties; understand relations between angles, side lengths, perimeters, surface areas, and volumes

Materials needed:
• copier paper for the booklets
• pencils, loose-leaf paper
• markers to print or computer time to type the definitions in the booklets

Can be used as teacher is introducing the basic concepts of geometry.

Page 26 - "Guess-and-Check" Problems

Students must know:

• how to write a story problem
• how to solve a problem using the "guess-and-check" strategy
• the step-by-step process of writing a problem that can be solved by the "guess-and-check" strategy

NCTM Standard - Problem Solving apply and adapt a variety of appropriate strategies to solve problems (for example: the "guess-and-check" strategy)

Materials needed:
• loose-leaf paper and pencils
• markers, if the students want to decorate the problems or write them out by hand

Can be used when reinforcing the strategies necessary to solve "guess-and-check" story problems.

Page 27 - Investing

Students must know:

• how to read the rise and fall of individual stocks in the newspaper or on the Internet
• how to make a recording chart
• how to make a graph from the data collected

NCTM Standards - Data Analysis and Probability and Connections formulate questions, design studies, and collect data; select, create, and use appropriate graphical representations of data; recognize and apply mathematics to contexts outside of mathematics

Materials needed:
• daily newspapers for each student
• loose-leaf paper, pencils
• graph paper and markers
• time to research on the Internet

Can be used when students need reinforcement in graphing skills, percent profit, and study of the rise and fall of stock prices.

Page 28 - Lunch Bag Volume

Students must know:

• how to find the volume of a lunch bag (rectangular prism)
• how to make a graph of the various volumes
• how to find the volume of the different kinds of food students may bring to school in their lunch bags
• how to make a model of a box or bag of their own design

NCTM Standards - Geometry and Connections develop strategies to determine volume of selected geometric figures; recognize and apply mathematics to contexts outside of mathematics

Materials needed:
• lots of different kinds of lunch bags or lunch boxes
• paper, pencils, rulers, and markers
• graph paper

Can be used when students are learning to find volumes of three-dimensional geometric shapes; also when studying nutrition.

Page 29 - Making a Division Game

Students must know:

• all the concepts of division (This is a great culminating project after a division chapter.)
• how to make a board game, and the components necessary to make an exciting board game (discussion of various board games will help them with this)
• how to write a very specific set of directions

NCTM Standards - Number and Operations and Connections compute (divide) fluently with whole numbers and decimals; recognize and apply mathematics to contexts outside of mathematics

Materials needed:
• one poster board, cut 20" x 20" for each group (or whatever size poster is available)
• many packets of small index cards
• markers
• clear set of directions to the game

Can be used as reinforcement of division of whole numbers and decimals.

TEACHER NOTES FOR *MATH PROJECT* PAGES (cont.)

Page 30 - Making a "Find the Shapes" House

Students must know:

- most geometric shapes and how to draw them
- how to use a compass and a protractor
- how to make circles when given the area or the circumference
- how to construct a 90˚ angle
- how to make an answer key

NCTM Standard - Geometry analyze properties of two-dimensional geometric shapes; understand relationships among areas of shapes

Materials needed:

- students will be given a partner with whom to exchange their completed houses
- one piece of art paper and one large poster board for each student
- geometric tools, protractor, compass, rulers, pencils, markers

Can be used at the end of a geometry unit where students have learned to identify basic geometric shapes, how to find their areas, and how to find the circumference and area of circles.

Page 31 - Making a Geometry Quiz

Students must know:

- how to write a multi-step story problem
- how to solve geometric story problems about geometric terms (It may be necessary to divide the geometry chapters into sections and assign one section to each pair of students.)
- how to make an answer key

NCTM Standard - Geometry describe, classify, and understand relationships among two- and three-dimensional objects; using defining properties; understand relations between angles, side lengths, perimeters, surface areas, and volumes

Materials needed:

- students must be assigned a partner
- loose-leaf paper or computer paper, pencil, rulers, yardsticks, meter sticks
- black or color fine-point markers

Can be used as the students complete their study of geometry, since they will have to include all aspects of geometry in this project. It can also be adapted to use after students have completed one area of geometry, for instance, lines, angles, and points.

Page 32 - Making a Multiplication Activity Pamphlet

Students must know:

- how to multiply whole numbers or decimal numbers or both
- the different kinds of activities found in the activity books kids take in the car on vacation
- the properties of multiplication
- how to write one-step, two-step, and multi-step problems

NCTM Standard - Number and Operations compute fluently

Materials needed:

- paper and pencil
- copier paper
- computer time
- a few samples of the activity books kids sometimes take in the car on vacation

Can be used when students need reinforcement in all areas of multiplication of whole numbers; also how to solve and write one-step, two-step, and multi-step story problems.

Page 33 - Math Manipulatives Lesson

Students must know:

- how to make a transparency either on a copy machine or by hand
- how to solve problems using manipulatives
- how to write simple problems that can be solved using manipulatives
- how to write a very clear set of rules to present to a class of younger students in order to teach a lesson to them

NCTM Standards - Number and Operations and Algebra compute fluently and use the associative and commutative properties of addition and multiplication, also the identity, zero, and distributive properties

Materials needed:

- lots of different manipulatives divided up into baggies to be passed to small groups of younger students (centimeter cubes, color tiles)
- lots of blank transparencies
- lots of transparency markers

Can be used as students are learning to use manipulatives to help them solve story problems; also, when students need to learn how to develop a teaching lesson for their own class or another class.

TEACHER NOTES FOR *MATH PROJECT* PAGES (cont.)

Page 34 - Pattern Story Problems

Students must know:

- how to solve a pattern story problem using a table or by drawing a simple picture
- how to calculate addition, subtraction, multiplication, and division of fractions
- how to write story problems involving patterns

NCTM Standard - Number and Operations
compute (fractions) fluently

> **Materials needed:**
> - paper and pencils
> - large paper, either large art paper or chart paper
> - markers

Can be used when students need reinforcement in problem solving involving patterns.

Page 35 - Percent of Commercial Time on TV

Students must know:

- how to use a timer or stopwatch
- how to make a recording chart
- how to calculate percents, for ex. 15 minutes is what percent of 60 minutes? 15/60 = 0.25 or 25%
- how to do problems involving hours and minutes

NCTM Standard - Number and Operations
understand ways of representing numbers and work flexibly with fractions, decimals, and percents

> **Materials needed:**
> - a television
> - a stopwatch or timer of some sort
> - recording charts
> - a large poster for each group of students (groups of 3 or 4)

Can be used when students need reinforcement in finding what percent one amount of time is of another amount of time.

Page 36 - Pictures Help Solve Problems

Students must know:

- how to calculate using whole numbers, fractions, or decimals, or all three (It can be teacher's choice.)
- how to draw a picture to help find the solution to a problem
- how to write multi-step story problems

NCTM Standard - Number and Operations
understand ways of representing numbers and work flexibly with fractions, decimals, and percents

> **Materials needed:**
> - paper and pencils
> - three large pieces of paper, one set per student
> - markers

Can be used when teaching the strategy of drawing out a picture to help solve a story problem; also practice writing these kinds of problems.

Page 37 - Planning a Garden

Students must know:

- how to choose items and calculate costs from a gardening catalog or a newspaper garden shop advertisement (done in small groups)
- how to calculate areas
- how to make a transparency either on a copy machine or by hand

NCTM Standards - Measurement and Problem Solving
understand and use units of measurement to measure area; use formulas to determine area of various shapes; draw a picture to solve a problem

> **Materials needed:**
> - paper, pencils, transparency markers
> - lots of transparencies copied with graph paper grids on them
> - lots of plant and seed catalogs

Can be used when students need reinforcement in dividing a space into specific areas; also budgeting costs when choosing plants for a garden.

Page 38 - Planning a School Supply Store

Students must know:

- how to choose items and calculate total costs from a catalog (done in small groups)
- how to choose items for a school supply store (What do students need?)
- how to calculate percent profit, ex. selling price as opposed to wholesale price (Wholesale price is what you paid for the item.)

NCTM Standard - Number and Operations
compute fluently; understand ways of representing numbers and work flexibly with fractions, decimals, and percents

> **Materials needed:**
> - lots of school supply catalogs
> - paper, pencils, markers, and calculators
> - large paper, like chart paper

Can be used to help with organizational skills and to learn how to order items from a catalog, how to order several items at a unit price, and then how to calculate percent profit between buying price and selling price.

TEACHER NOTES FOR *MATH PROJECT* PAGES (cont.)

Page 39 - Planning a Vacation

Students must know:

- how to work in a small group to complete a task
- how to calculate miles per hour, distance traveled, and miles per gallon of gasoline
- how to use a distance scale on a map
- general costs of fast food, gasoline, motel rooms
- how to write an hour-by-hour schedule of a day's activities

NCTM Standards - Number and Operations and Connections   compute fluently and recognize and apply mathematics to contexts outside of mathematics

Materials needed:

- paper and pencils
- maps or atlases of states or maps of the United States
- large paper, chart paper, or poster board

Can be used when students need to learn to plan a vacation using a certain budget, how to use a distance scale, and how to calculate miles per gallon of fuel.

Page 40 - Positive and Negative Numbers

Students must know:

- how to write story problems
- how to add and subtract negative numbers
- how to draw a picture to solve a problem
- how to make a table to solve a problem
- how to do a "work-backwards" problem

NCTM Standards - Number and Operations and Problem Solving   understand relationships among numbers; develop and analyze algorithms for computing integers; apply and adapt a variety of problem-solving strategies to solve problems

Materials needed:

- paper and pencils
- access to transparencies and transparency pens
- chart paper or poster board

Can be used when students have just been introduced to adding and subtracting negative numbers; also, how to solve and write complex story problems.

Page 41 - Probability and Prediction

Students must know:

- how to design a probability test, like tossing a coin to see if you get heads or tails
- how to make a recording chart to record the results of their tests
- how to analyze the data to form a prediction about what will happen if you did the same test over again

NCTM Standard - Data Analysis and Probability   formulate questions, design studies, and collect data; select, create, and use appropriate graphical representations of data; make conjectures based on their studies

Materials needed:

- coins, dice, spinners, and different-colored little cubes
- graph paper, paper, and pencils

Can be used when students are working on a probability unit and are learning to use probability data to predict the outcome of future data collection, then to test their second trial and compare the outcome to their first set of data.

Page 42 - Producing a Math Survey

Students must know:

- how to write questions about math that have a "yes" or "no" response
- how to make a recording chart
- how to write a letter to a teacher to ask permission to survey his/her class
- how to calculate percentage of the answers to each question
- how to convert recorded data into a bar graph

NCTM Standard - Data Analysis and Probability   formulate questions, design studies, and collect data; select, create, and use appropriate graphical representations of data

Materials needed:

- paper and pencils
- graph paper and markers
- computer time to write letters and to make a copy of the survey
- a way to make copies for a class in order to survey the students

Can be used when students are learning how to write a good survey, collect data on the survey, analyze the results, and present the data in percentages on a bar graph or circle graph.

TEACHER NOTES FOR *MATH PROJECT* PAGES (cont.)

Page 43 - Ratios of Age to Height

Students must know:

- how to write a ratio
- how to make a recording chart with student names, a column to record ages, and another for heights
- how to find the average age and height of one age group
- how to make a transparency (optional)

NCTM Standard - Data Analysis and Probability

formulate questions, design studies, and collect data; select, create, and use appropriate graphical representations of data; find, use, and interpret data

Materials needed:
- pencil and paper
- small graph paper and large graph paper, or chart paper, poster board, etc.
- transparencies
- markers and transparency pens

Can be used when students are learning how to set up ratios and when they need practice collecting data and calculating averages; also they will make bar graphs of their findings.

Page 44 - Splendid Story Problems

Students must know:

- how to write a story problem
- how to do all calculations using whole numbers, fractions, decimals, and percents, or any skill you would like to reinforce
- the difference between one-step, two-step, and multi-step story problems

NCTM Standard - Number and Operations

compute fluently; understand ways of representing numbers; work flexibly with fractions, decimals, and percents

Materials needed:
- paper and pencil for first drafts
- computer time for each student

Can be used to reinforce writing story problems and the calculation of whole numbers, decimals, fractions, and even geometry.

Page 45 - Story Problems With Combinations

Students must know:

- how to write and solve problems involving combinations of things, like ice cream flavors, pizza toppings, choices on a restaurant menu, etc.
- how to make a handwritten transparency, or how to make a copy of the problems on the computer that can be copied as a transparency

NCTM Standard - Problem Solving   apply and adapt

a variety of problem-solving strategies to solve problems

Materials needed:
- paper and pencils for the first drafts
- computer time or transparencies and transparency pens

Can be used when practicing solving and writing story problems involving combinations of things.

Page 46 - *Titanic* Brain Teasers

Students must know:

- how to write complicated story problems that can be called "Brain Teasers"
- how to do Internet searches to find data about the ship *Titanic*
- how to use encyclopedias to find information, or how to use encyclopedias online

NCTM Standards - Number and Operations and Connections   compute fluently and recognize and apply

mathematics to contexts outside of mathematics

Materials needed:
- paper and pencils for the first draft of Brain Teasers
- computer time and use of a printer for each small group

Can be used to help students research data about the great ship *Titanic* in the library or on the Internet, and then to form story problems using the data they find.

TEACHER NOTES FOR *MATH PROJECT* PAGES (cont.)

Page 47 - Wallpapering vs. Painting a Room

Students must know:

- how to find the area of wall space in a room, minus doors and windows; it is good to let the students find the total wall space of their classroom the week before introducing this project
- how to calculate wages when given $ per hour
- how to calculate the price of wallpaper to cover an entire room
- painting is cheaper

NCTM Standards - Measurement and Problem Solving understand and use units of measurement to measure area; use formulas to determine area of various shapes; apply and adapt a variety of problem-solving strategies to solve problems

Materials needed:

- paper, pencils, and calculators
- chart paper (to write calculated costs for wallpapering and painting)
- markers

Can be done along with the introduction of finding the area of rectangular shapes and to help students find which method of renewing a room would be cheaper.

Page 48 - "Who Am I?" Game

Students must know:

- how to write clues for a "Who Am I?" game, starting with the most general clue first, and then becoming more specific. The last clue is the one that gives the answer away. (Samples of clues are given on the student sheet.)

For this lesson, the chapters on Geometry in the textbook must be divided into 3- or 4-page sections, and each pair of students is to be assigned a set of these pages.

NCTM Standard - Geometry analyze properties of three-dimensional shapes and develop arguments about geometric relationships

Materials needed:

- paper and pencils
- about 20 or 30 large index cards for every pair of students
- markers to print clues
- resource books with additional geometry definitions

Can be done as the teacher covers a geometry unit, or it can be done as a culmination of the entire unit.

Page 49 - "Work-Backwards" Problems

Students must know:

- how to write and solve "work-backwards" problems by using the information given at the END of the problem and then working toward the beginning of the problem to find the solution
- how to write simple "work-backwards" problems
- how to act out the solution to a problem

NCTM Standard - Problem Solving apply and adapt a variety of problem-solving strategies to solve problems

Materials needed:

- paper and pencils for first draft problems
- poster board
- markers

Can be done to reinforce and give students practice in solving and then writing their own "work-backwards" story problems.

Page 50 - Writing About Long Journeys

Students must know:

- how to use their social studies book, the Internet, or the library to find specific numeric information about the journeys of some of the great explorers
- how to write story problems
- how to draw a map with a map legend

NCTM Standards - Problem Solving and Connections apply and adapt a variety of problem-solving strategies to solve problems and recognize and apply mathematics to contexts outside of mathematics

Materials needed:

- class time for research, library or computer research time
- paper and pencils for rough drafts
- poster board or chart paper for each small group
- colored markers

Can be done in correlation with the study of the great explorers and to reinforce research skills to collect data about these explorers and their journeys; also, the students must develop story problems using this data.

A Playground Game Design

ASSIGNMENTS AND GUIDELINES:

This week, you will be working with a group of three or four students to design a playground game that children would like to play at recess. The playground game you design must be age-appropriate for the children in your school. You are to decide upon fast games that children can play at recess and allow a specific area for your game. Your assignments are as follows:

1. Draw a rough draft and then a final design of the game on a large piece of poster board or chart paper.
2. Decide how much area is needed for the game. For example, how long and how wide will this hopscotch game be? Place measurements for the game on the paper as shown below.
3. Make your game colorful, challenging, and interesting.
4. Decide on a scoring method, and include it on the drawing.
5. Make a list of rules to be followed when playing the game. If the game is for 5- and 6-year-olds, the teacher can read the rules to the students.
6. Be prepared to share the game with the class. Perhaps you could draw the actual game outdoors on the asphalt in chalk for art class on a nice, warm day.

← 10 feet →

Pirate Ship Beanbag Toss

18 feet

throw line

Rules for the Beanbag Toss
1. Stand behind the throw line to toss the bags.
2. Each person throws the bag one time per turn.
3. When someone's score reaches 15, they are the winner.

Scoring Method for Beanbag Toss
1. If a bag lands on a sail, it is 1 point.
2. If a bag lands in a big window, it is 2 points.
3. If a bag lands on a small window, it is 3 points.
4. If a bag lands on the pirate, it is 5 points.

Algebraic Equations

ASSIGNMENTS AND GUIDELINES:

This week, you will be writing three story problems with a partner. The problems will be simple and will follow the pattern shown below. After you complete the written story problem, then you must develop an equation from the problem as shown below. You will write out each problem on large paper along with the equation, and whenever possible, you will write an explanation of why you formulated the equation as you did. Each of the three problems must follow the directives below:

1. One of the problems must involve addition.For example: Carlos had some bananas. Benjamin had five **more** bananas than Carlos. Together, they had 15 bananas. How many did each of them have? (In this problem, the word *more* indicates addition.)

2. The second and third problems must involve the multiplication process. For example: Manuel had some baseball cards. Marcus had three times the number of baseball cards as Manuel. Together, they had 24 cards. How many did each of them have?

SAMPLE PROBLEM:
Let's develop an equation for the addition problem above:

We will let the letter n represent José's bananas.
We will let the quantity $(n+5)$ equal Carlos's bananas.
Now, we will write an equation from this:

$$n \quad + \quad (n+5) \quad = \quad 15$$
(Carlos's bananas) + (Benjamin's bananas) =   total

To solve this:

$n + (n + 5) = 15$ then, $2n + 5 = 15$ then, $2n = 15 - 5$
then, $2n = 10$ and finally, $n = 5$

Analyzing Graphs

ASSIGNMENT ONE:

This week we will be looking at, studying, and then writing about the graphs you acquired. These are your goals for the week:

1. Look through the five or six graphs provided by your teacher and choose the one that is best for this assignment.
2. After you choose the graph you need, develop ten questions that you could ask someone about the graph. Write these questions neatly on a piece of loose-leaf paper.
3. On a second piece of loose-leaf, write the answers to your questions.
4. On a third piece of loose-leaf, explain the graph and tell what the graph is communicating to you. Why did the person who made the graph go to the trouble of making it?
5. On the third piece of loose-leaf, tell how you could improve the graph if you had all the colors, pens, markers, computer software, etc., you needed at your fingertips.
6. Exchange the questions and graph with a partner, and have him/her answer your questions.

ASSIGNMENT TWO:

Next, you will choose another graph. You are to compose five good story problems using the information presented on the graph. The story problems can incorporate any process: addition, subtraction, multiplication, or division of whole numbers, decimals, fractions, or percents. The problems are to be done on loose-leaf and then revised and done in final draft on the computer, if one is available. The following shows two examples of problems developed about a graph:

> Using the graph entitled: "ANNUAL SALARIES OF MIDDLE-INCOME AMERICANS," please estimate the average income of all types of workers. Then find the actual average using data from the graph.

> Using the graph entitled: "ENDANGERED SPECIES ON THE EARTH," calculate the difference between the endangered animals that come from the rain forests as opposed to those coming from the deserts.

Finally, give your questions to a partner.

ASSIGNMENT THREE:

1. Choose one of the graphs that you think you could improve, and then plan how you would change the graph.
2. Secondly, get a large piece of chart paper or very large graph paper and make the graph over.
3. Present the graph to your class, and explain to them why you chose this type of presentation.

Bicycle Trip Plan

ASSIGNMENTS AND GUIDELINES:

This week, you will be working with a partner to plan a 250-mile, one-way bicycle trip from your city or area to another city or area. You will be in a simulated cross-country bicycle race, and you will be permitted to travel on any major highway without danger of traffic. (Remember, this is a "pretend" race.) You will calculate distances by using an average of 10 miles per hour.

Your assignment, therefore, is to plan out the distances you will travel each day, to list the time schedule you will follow, and estimate the arrival time and date. The rules for the race are as follows:

1. You must travel as far as you can before 5:00 P.M. each day. Then, you must stop to rest for the night. (You are carrying a small lightweight tent in a backpack for sleeping.)

2. You may use any roadway available.

2. You are only permitted to rest until 7:00 A.M. By then, you must have eaten breakfast and gotten back on the road.

3. You must stop during the day for an additional two hours for lunch, dinner, and a nap.

4. The winner will be the person who arrives at the destination first, but you must be honest and follow the rules. To complete the assignment, you will need several maps of the area and the areas about 250 miles from your starting point. You will need a large piece of paper to record your schedule.

SAMPLE RACE PLAN:

Departure date: June 10   7:00 A.M.   Distance: 250 miles
Depart from: Pittsburgh, Pennsylvania   Speed: approximately 10 mph
Destination: Washington, D.C.

Schedule for June 10

1. To leave the Golden Triangle in Pittsburgh at 7:00 A.M. Travel east on Route 22 for approximately 20 miles to get on the Pennsylvania Turnpike at 9:00 A.M.

2. Enter the turnpike and arrive at Mt. Pleasant, about 30 miles from Pittsburgh, at 12:00 P.M. for a one-hour lunch break and a short nap.

3. 1:00 P.M. leave Mt. Pleasant, go to Somerset, which is 30 miles. Arrive at 4:00 P.M. Plan for bicycle tire change and dinner after arriving in Somerset at 4:00 P.M., study the trip for tomorrow, and then sleep in the tent.

Budgeting

ASSIGNMENTS AND GUIDELINES:

This week, you will be working with a partner to develop two types of budgets. Here is an outline of your assignments for the week.

1. Develop a budget for a teenager that will help him/her develop financial responsibility.
   a. The teenager gets an $80.00 monthly allowance. From that amount, he/she must pay for all of the items he/she wants, such as movies, high-tech gadgets, makeup, new games, etc.
   b. Convert the amounts you have allotted to percents and place these on a circle graph on large paper. (Use the ideas provided for you in the teenage budget rectangle below to help you.)
2. Secondly, devise a budget for a family household. (It may help if you get an idea of the fractional amount your own family allots for each category shown below.)
   a. Using an imaginary monthly income of $5,000.00, you will decide on the money amounts the family of four can allot for the things they need.
   b. After you are satisfied with the budget, you will convert the amounts of the budget to percentages and design a circle graph.
   c. Complete both of the graphs and share them with the class.

TEENAGE BUDGET

These are some items teens may place in their budget.

1. movie tickets
2. school supplies
3. sports games
4. gasoline
5. hair and beauty items
6. snacks/candy
7. hobbies
8. clothing

FAMILY BUDGET

1. mortgage
2. car payments
3. car insurance
4. gasoline
5. electric bill
6. charge card bills
7. savings
8. food bill
9. dancing or swimming lessons
10. instrument rental
11. spending money
12. emergency fund
13. entertaining
14. clothing

Building a Dog Area

ASSIGNMENTS AND GUIDELINES:

This week, you will be creating an outside, fenced-in area where a dog could be kept on nice days. You are trying to keep costs as low as possible, so you must plan carefully. Here are assignments for the week:

1. Build a fenced-in dog area for the least amount of money.

2. Buy a piece of land that costs $4.00 a square foot.

3. Erect posts and a four-foot-high chain link fence, the kind that are on most school properties.

4. Buy bags of dry pack cement that harden when mixed with water, one bag to pour around every three posts. (This keeps the posts solidly in the ground.)

5. After you have designed your area, calculate the costs. To do this, get a copy of a local hardware or lumber company's advertisements. The objective is to spend the least amount of money that you can to make a sturdy area.

6. Draw your area on one side of a large piece of art paper and the costs on the other side. Be prepared to share with the class.

---

1. Remember, you will need one post for every four feet of the length of each side of your fence. You may have more posts, but not less.
2. Do not forget the corner posts.
3. You may want to consider the advantages of a square area, a round area, a triangular area, or a rectangular area.
4. Don't forget the tools you will need for this project; you must purchase them.

Collecting Data

ASSIGNMENTS AND GUIDELINES:

This week, you will be working in either cooperative learning groups or with a partner to complete the following:

1. Devise three "tests" or surveys to conduct in the next two or three days. Perform one test at a time, record the data, and then go on to the next test. Here is an idea for a test your group could do:
   a. You could have each member of your group jump rope for 30 seconds to see how many times his or her feet leave the ground in that 30-second period.
   b. Each member of your group will do this 30-second jump-rope exercise 3 times.
   c. You will then record your results on recording charts like this:

Name	Trial 1	Trial 2	Trial 3

2. Choose one set of the most interesting data, and construct a large bar graph for that data.

3. Then, on a piece of chart paper or newsprint in large printing, tell about your graph. Tell what happened in each trial, to each person. This is the order you should use to describe your graph:
   a. tell the title of your graph.
   b. explain what is shown on the vertical axis.
   c. explain what is shown on the horizontal axis.
   d. explain the key you may have made to clarify your data.

4. On the assigned day, you will share with the class: the title of your test, the bar graph, and the explanation of the graph.

HERE IS A LIST OF IDEAS FOR GATHERING DATA:

1. Measure the pulse rate of each person in your group, first, at rest; second, after they do 20 jumping jacks; and third, 2 minutes after stopping the jumping jacks.

2. Survey your class or another class to ask which music group they prefer. You could also survey their favorite TV show, computer game, food, or snack, etc.

3. See how fast each person could run 20 meters. (Remember to test each person 3 times.)

4. Measure how long each person in your group can dribble a basketball, or how many bounces the ball makes while being dribbled until the person loses control of it.

5. Here is an example of a graph to help you:

TITLE: HOW MANY BASKETS CAN WE MAKE IN 60 SECONDS?

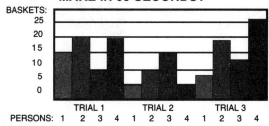

Comparing Grass Growth vs. Price

ASSIGNMENTS AND GUIDELINES:

This week, you will compare different types of grass seed and see which grass seed grows best for the price. To do this project, you will work with a partner. You will need four types of grass seed. Before you begin, please note the cost of the seed per ounce.

1. You will need four small containers (each one about the size of the bottom of a plastic gallon milk container).
2. You will need dirt to fill each of the containers to a depth of at least two inches of soil. Store-bought soil is best for this.
3. You will need 25 of each kind of grass seed.
4. You will need a measuring cup for watering.
5. Label the growing containers with permanent marker or masking tape, showing the particular grass seed that will be planted in that container.
6. Finally, you will need a recording chart like the one below to record the data that you will collect.
7. Plant the seed just under the level of the soil and water the entire surface of the soil with 1/2 cup of water. Continue to water the plants every other day with 1/4 cup water. Record the number of seeds that germinate or sprout in each container. Graph your results. You may want to calculate the percentages of the grass seed that germinate. Divide the number of seeds that sprout each day by 25. Move the decimal two places to the right, and you will have the percentage!

RECORDING CHART FOR <u>NUMBER</u> OF SEEDS GERMINATING				
date	seeds #1 $___/oz.	seeds #2 $___/oz.	seeds #3 $___/oz.	seeds #4 $___/oz.
month-day-year	# of Seeds	# of Seeds	# of Seeds	# of Seeds
10-15-12	3			

Comparing Prices and Ingredients of Cereals

ASSIGNMENTS AND GUIDELINES:

This week, you will bring as many kinds of cereal boxes as you can find at home to school. Take the cereal out of the box before bringing the box to school. You will be working with a partner to analyze the nutritional facts and price per ounce of four or five cereals. Here are the assignments for the week:

1. Use the "Nutrition Facts" listed on the cereal boxes to help you make a poster similar to the one below. Calculate the price per ounce of each cereal.
2. Study the nutrition facts on the side of the box and place the number of grams or milligrams of each ingredient in the correct row.
3. After you have listed the nutrition facts, develop a bar graph of each cereal you studied. One idea is to rank the cereal with the most harmful ingredients (fat, sodium, and sugar) and the one with the most healthy ingredients (dietary fiber and protein) on a transparency graph. Share your results with the class.

A Sample Chart

	Bobbie's Wheat Flakes $0.31 oz.	Chucky's Corn Chunks $0.19 oz.	Sam's Granola $0.52 oz.	Crunchy Corn Pops $0.32 oz.	Cheap Crisps $0.15 oz.
Calories					
Calories from fat					
Total fat					
Saturated fat					
Polyunsaturated fat					
Monounsaturated fat					
Cholesterol					
Sodium					
Potassium					
Total carbohydrates					
Dietary fiber					
Soluble fiber					
Sugars					
Other carbohydrates					
Protein					

Conducting a Metric Olympics

ASSIGNMENTS AND GUIDELINES:

This week, you will be working with a group to design three games for a metric competition that we will have next week on a nice day when we can go outdoors. Your assignments are as follows:

1. Design the three games, one using the metric measurements for volume (capacity), one using the metric measurements for weight, and the last using metric length.

2. Make a list of all the materials needed for your game.

3. Make charts to record each contestant's measurements, and make sure that each member of your team has a job to do on the actual day of the Olympics.

4. Write a set of rules to be read and followed by the contestants as they compete.

5. Make a banner for your game, which may be made on the computer or by hand.

6. Provide a map of the school grounds to show where your game will be located.

7. As a class, we will make a schedule that will have half of the groups running their games, while the other half of the groups actually "play" the games; then, for the second half of the time, we will switch.

SAMPLE GAME IDEAS:

Capacity or *Volume* game ideas:
1. How fast can you fill a 2-liter container with water using 100-milliliter cups?
2. How fast can you fill a 100-milliliter container using a dropper?
3. How many cups can fit into a liter container? Who can fill the container the fastest?

Weight game ideas:
1. How many pieces of gravel equal 1 kilogram?
2. How fast can you weigh 10 grams of cotton balls? (one at a time)
3. How fast can you get 100 grams of paper clips onto a metric scale? (one at a time)

Length game ideas:
1. How far can you throw a cotton ball? (in six tries)
2. How far can you jump? (in three tries)
3. How long of a paper clip chain can you make in two minutes?

Connecting Decimals and Fractions

ASSIGNMENTS AND GUIDELINES:

This week, you will be choosing between two projects. The first choice is to make a "Connect-the-Dots" circle. Your circle will be a kind of puzzle. There is an example in the illustration below. The other choice is to make a small Concentration game using fractions and their equivalent decimals. An example of this is shown at the right. Whichever you choose, after the project is complete, you will be exchanging it with another person. Each assignment is described below.

CONNECT-THE-DOT PAGE

1. Make at least 8 to 16 pairs of fractions and their equivalent decimals.
2. On white art paper, draw a large circle, at least 8 inches in diameter.
3. Now place 16 to 32 dots all around the circle, and place the pairs of fractions and decimals on opposite sides from each other at each point around the circle.
4. The person who solves the puzzle will connect each equivalent fraction with its decimal pair with a straight line.
5. When the puzzles are complete, return them to the owner to be checked.

CONCENTRATION GAME SAMPLE:

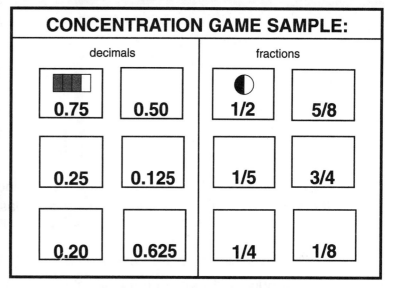

decimals		fractions	
0.75	0.50	1/2	5/8
0.25	0.125	1/5	3/4
0.20	0.625	1/4	1/8

CONCENTRATION GAME

1. Get 15 small index cards.
2. Cut them all in half.
3. Make up 15 sets of matching equivalent fractions and decimals. (ex. 1/2 = 0.5)
4. Place each fraction or decimal on the card halves.
5. Draw a <u>picture</u> of the fraction or decimal piece right above the fraction or decimal using a pizza, a candy bar, a tenths chart, etc.
6. Write clear directions to your game, making sure that when the students lay out the cards, they place them FACE DOWN on the playing table or floor.
7. Finally, exchange your game with another person.

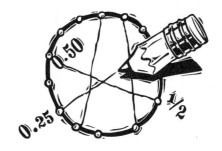

Coordinate Puzzles

ASSIGNMENTS AND GUIDELINES:

This week, you will be making two coordinate puzzles for another student in the class. Here is a list of the assignments for the next few days:

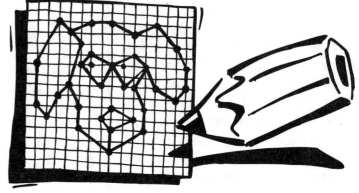

1. Make two drawings on two separate pieces of 4-quadrant graph paper, like that shown below.

2. Simplify each of these drawings so that you can attach a coordinate name to certain points on the drawings, similar to the illustration at the right.

3. On your original drawing, print a set of coordinates for each dot on your drawing.

4. On another sheet of paper, list just the two sets of coordinates for your drawings, starting at one point and continuing around the perimeter of the drawing. Label each set of coordinates: Drawing 1, Drawing 2.

5. Exchange just the coordinates with a partner and see if you can reproduce each other's drawings.

6. On the assigned day, be prepared to share each of your puzzle solutions with the class.

7. If time allows, choose the best puzzle and make it two or three times the size of the original. How do your coordinates change?

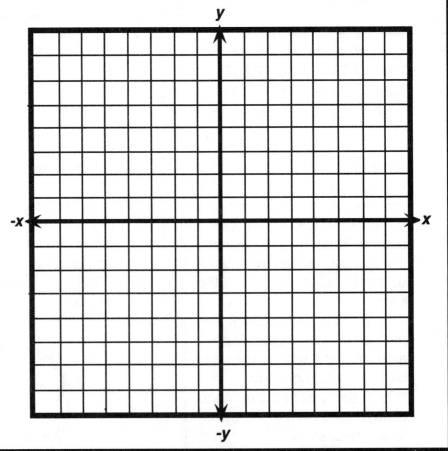

Dancing Geometric Shapes

ASSIGNMENTS AND GUIDELINES:

This week, you will be working with a small rectangle to learn geometry moves. Here is the assignment:

1. Use a piece of coordinate graph paper (with squares that are one-half-inch wide) and a small rectangle cut from graph paper (also with 1/2-inch squares) measuring 2 inches long by 1/2-inch wide.

2. Label each corner of the little shape with letters A, B, C, and D on each corner on both the top and the underside of the rectangle. A, B, C, and D will be in the same corners on both sides like this:

A	top	C
B	side	D

C	bottom	A
D	side	B

3. On the x- and y-axis, label all the coordinates on the coordinate paper: +1, +2, +3, and -1, -2, -3, etc., as shown in the picture below.

4. Place the shape on the top right corner of the coordinate paper, and move it to the bottom left corner of the paper using the moves listed below.

5. Now make up your own directions for moving the shape down the piece of coordinate graph paper. Write a set of directions for each move that you make. Use the set of directions below as an example.

6. Give a partner your set of directions and the little shape you made, to see if he/she can follow your exact path from the top to the bottom of the page.

VOCABULARY TO USE:

1. translation, which means to slide
2. reflection, which means to flip
3. rotation, which means to turn

A SAMPLE SET OF DIRECTIONS:

1. Start with your rectangle in the vertical position, with corner "A" right in the corner at coordinates (+7,+7).

2. Move by translation so that the same "A" corner is at coordinates (+7,+5).

3. Make a reflection move over the x-axis.

4. Rotate the shape counterclockwise 90°, around coordinate point (+6,-5).

5. Make a translation move directly south so that corner "B" is at coordinates (+6,-7).

6. Make a reflection move over axis at "+1."

7. Make a translation move 3 spaces to the left, so the "B" is at the coordinates, (-7,-7).

Designing the Perfect Classroom

ASSIGNMENTS AND GUIDELINES:

This week, you will pretend that you have been asked by the Department of Education to design and furnish the classroom of your dreams. You will be given an unlimited budget for this classroom design. However, you must show all of your calculations at the end of the project development. Here is a list of requirements for the week:

1. Work with a group to design a classroom that students would dream about.

2. Decide what pieces of the present classroom should be retained.

3. Then decide what is going into the room, and then calculate the space you need. To do this, you may need to review office and school supply catalogs. Your classroom may be as large or as small as you wish.

4. At the end of the week, you should have three (or four) items to share with the class:
   a. all the furniture you need
   b. all the technology you need
   c. the costs and totals of the above items
   d. If there is time, obtain some cardboard and make a model or architectural drawing of the classroom.

SOME IDEAS THAT MAY HELP YOU:

- The first thing you want to do is to decide what aspects of a classroom are the most important.
- Decide on the floor area and shape that you want for your classroom.
- Perhaps you would like tables instead of desks.
- You may want to have study lamps at the tables or desks.
- Where and how will you include technology in the room?
- How about having a living room corner, where there is a place for a sofa and a few comfortable chairs?
- How about a pillow corner on the floor?
- Interview your teachers to find out what they would like to have in the classroom, and include some of their ideas.
- What kinds of furniture (other than desks, tables, and chairs) will you need to support your educational environment?

Developing a Summer Business

ASSIGNMENTS AND GUIDELINES:

This week, you will be working in cooperative learning groups to make all the plans for starting your own summer business. You can start any kind of business you want as long as you plan carefully. These are the planning steps you are to follow. Good luck!

1. The first step in planning a business is to develop one that will make a profit and that you will enjoy doing. Choose a business that you can perform from your own home.

2. The business you plan will employ exactly the number of persons in your group (three or four).

3. After you choose the kind of business you want to start, make a list of materials that you will need and how you will buy these materials. (Will you take out a loan?)

4. Next, do some research on prices. Depending on the type of business you want to start, your prices will come from stores or catalogs. A good idea is to divide the responsibilities of finding the best price for each item you need to buy among all group members.

5. Divide the various jobs among your group. For instance, if you are going to write and publish small books that could be rented by the students in your school next year, you must have writers, editors, paper-cutters, binders, and marketing agents to go to the classrooms to introduce and rent out the books. Decide the salaries that each person will receive. Will the writers get the same as binders?

6. Record your plan in a neat, organized manner on a long strip of poster board as shown at the right. Try to list all your plans carefully. Make sure you don't forget the details!

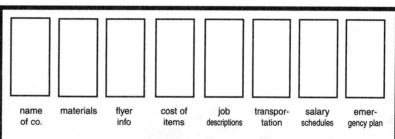

| name of co. | materials | flyer info | cost of items | job descriptions | transpor-tation | salary schedules | emer-gency plan |

IDEAS FOR PLANNING A BUSINESS:

You could start a grocery delivery business in the area near your homes. Here is a plan for this type of business:

1. Make a flyer advertising your business. In the flyer, have a map showing the blocks that you and your partners' business covers. Have the cost of delivery of one bag of groceries, two bags of groceries, etc. Have a list of your phone numbers with the best times to call for a delivery.

2. Construct a wagon that can be pulled by your bicycle, or your partners' bicycles, in which to haul the groceries.

3. Decide how you will handle the money. For instance, will you pay for the entire order of groceries and then get the payment plus delivery costs from the client, or will you pick up the money from the client, go to the store, and then give the client his/her change and present your bill for delivery?

4. How will you handle the profits? Will you have a bank account? How often will the partners get paid?

Draw a Diagram to Solve a Problem

ASSIGNMENTS AND GUIDELINES:

This week, you will be writing and illustrating story problems that can be solved by drawing a diagram. At least three of the problems must involve fractions, and all will be solved using graph paper. You will work with your partner to do the following:

1. Make up five story problems that can be solved by drawing a diagram on graph paper. (Sample problems are written below.)
2. Write the problems as a group, revise, and edit them, and then print each problem with marker in the upper half of a large piece of chart paper.
3. On the lower half of the paper, draw and color a picture to illustrate the solution.
4. On the assigned day, share the problems with the class.

Some ideas for problems with diagrams would be:

1. A caterpillar climbs three inches up a large tree each day and falls down $1\frac{1}{4}$ inches each day. If the tree is 4 feet tall, on which day will it reach the top?
2. A baker baked 10 chocolate chip cookies on Monday, 3 dozen on Thursday, $4\frac{1}{2}$ dozen on Friday, and 45 on Saturday. On Monday, he sold half of what he made. On Thursday, he sold a third. On Friday, he sold a half of what he made, and on Saturday, he sold $\frac{2}{5}$. How many cookies did he have to eat on Saturday night?

SAMPLE PROBLEM:

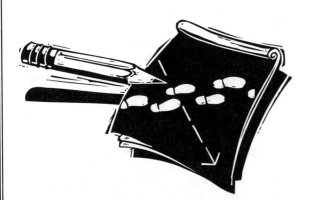

Charlie was at a party. He asked if there was any more soda. The host, Ginny, said that the soda was in the basement. Charlie asked her if she wanted him to go down to get some, and she said, "That would be great, but there is no light in our basement, and you have to find the soda by counting your steps." Charlie was pretty good at directions, so he listened and immediately put to memory what she said, which was: "Go to the bottom of the stairs, take five steps directly perpendicular to the bottom step. Turn to your right, and take 23 steps forward after you have turned. Turn to your left exactly 90° once again, and take 12 steps directly in front of you. Turn 90° to your left, and take 3 steps. Then make a 90° turn to your left and go 14 steps. Turn right, go 15 steps, and the soda will be at your feet. Got it?" she asked. "Sure, I got it, but I know a much shorter way to get the soda," he answered. Can you figure out Charlie's method? Use graph paper to find the solution.

Drawing Proportionate Figures

ASSIGNMENTS AND GUIDELINES:

This week, you will be drawing a figure that is made from any geometric shapes that you wish. There is only one rule. All lines making up the shape must be straight. Here are the assignments for the week:

1. Obtain a large piece of white drawing paper, preferably 24" by 18".
2. Divide the paper in half. On the left side of the paper, draw a simple figure that fits into about a six-inch square. The figure must lend itself to geometric shapes, like a robot or a building with windows.
3. Make your shape simple, because you will exchange it with another person and that person will draw the figure exactly the same, only larger, and to exact proportion.

To set up a proportion and solve:
1. Find the length of the left side of the small figure and place it over the width of the figure. ex. 5"/4"
2. Determine how large you want your second figure to be and draw the left side. Measure the length of that side, and place that in a fraction over the unknown width of the larger figure. ex. 8"/n
3. Place the two fractions side by side like this:

$$\frac{5"}{4"} = \frac{8"}{n}$$

and cross-multiply, then divide, to find the unknown length. 8 x 4 = 32
32 ÷ 5 = 6.4" Therefore, the width of the large figure has to be 6.4 inches to be exactly proportional to the small figure. Set up a proportion for all the lengths and widths of each line making up the small figure and the large figure.

4. When your partner has finished the drawing, share your picture with the class.

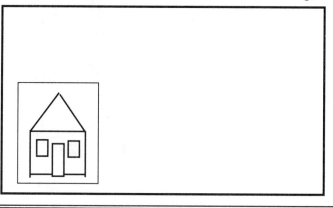
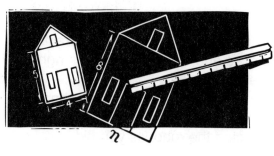

Fractional Robots

ASSIGNMENTS AND GUIDELINES:

1. This week, you will cut two robots out of fractional parts of square pieces of paper. First, make a little first draft robot out of paper measuring 20 cm by 20 cm. Then make the final robot out of heavy stock paper measuring 40 cm by 40 cm.
2. Make the robots out of the shapes as follows:
   a. Use $\frac{1}{4}$ of the original square to make one small square.
   b. Draw two long rectangles that are each $\frac{1}{8}$ of the original square.
   c. Draw two triangles that are each $\frac{1}{16}$ of the original square.
   d. Draw one more rectangle that is $\frac{4}{32}$ of the large piece.
   e. Divide the rest of the square up as you like.
3. Color the shapes as requested in the box below.
4. It is extremely important to draw and then color the shapes before cutting anything out on both of your robots.
5. After you cut out the pieces, glue the little robot shapes down on art paper and the final robot shapes down on posterboard.

COLORING DIRECTIONS:

Color the robot as follows:

1. 25% has to be red
2. 25% has to be green
3. 12.5% has to be blue
4. 12.5% has to be orange
5. 20% has to be yellow
6. 5% has to be black

After your robot is glued down to the poster, label all the fractional pieces and color percentages right <u>on</u> the poster.

Be prepared to share the poster with the class and tell why you constructed the robot as you did.

Fractional Floor Plans

ASSIGNMENTS AND GUIDELINES:

This week, you will be working with a partner to do the following assignments:

1. Construct the floor plan of a two-story house with no basement. The house may be a free-standing home or a townhouse.
2. Since you are only have a $200,000 budget, calculate carefully.
3. Each square foot of the house costs roughly $125.
4. Study the floor plan example you received to help you plan the area of each room. Don't forget to have a central hall on each floor to connect the rooms.

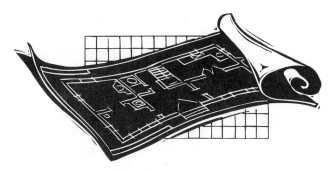

5. After you sketch the general plan of the house, do a small floor plan on centimeter graph paper. You will need several sheets of graph paper. Let each square centimeter equal one square foot. You should have two floor plans, a first floor and a second floor. <u>The rooms must be typical of a family home</u>.
6. Give your floor plan to another group. This group will make up ten story problems (with answer key), involving the space of the house, using addition and subtraction of fractions. The group will then return the floor plans to the original owners, and the original owners will solve the problems.

SAMPLE PROBLEMS:

1. Someone wants your floor plans to build the house that your group has designed. However, they have a grandma who has just come to live with them, and they would like to change part of the house design to include an apartment for her, i.e., a living room, bedroom, kitchen, and a bathroom. Show the new plan, determine the area of each room, and calculate the fraction of her area of the whole house.
2. What fractional part of the entire house is the living room, dining room, and kitchen?
3. What fractional part of the first floor is the kitchen?
4. Adding all of the bedroom areas together, what fraction of the whole house is the bedrooms?

Fractionated Fairy Tales

ASSIGNMENTS AND GUIDELINES:

This week, you will be writing story problems that are based on fairy tales. They may be short sections of a fairy tale, or you may become ambitious and make a long story problem out of a tale. (You may ask your teacher to adapt the requirements listed below if you decide to write one long, complicated problem instead of the short ones.) The following is a list of your assignments for the week:

1. Write five multi-step story problems based on fairy tales and fairy-tale characters.
2. These fairy-tale story problems may involve one or several of the processes of addition, subtraction, multiplication, and division.
3. Your problems should require operations involving whole numbers, fractions, decimals, percents, or any combinations of these.
4. Write your problems in draft form on loose-leaf paper. Then, transfer the problems in large print (at least $\frac{3}{4}$-inch tall) to chart paper.
5. On the reverse side of the chart paper, work out the solutions for each of the problems. It is vital that you show exactly how you found the solution to each problem. Ask your teacher if you can consult with a partner to help you with the solution if you have difficulty with it.
6. Be prepared to share your best problems with the class.

EXAMPLE:

1. Once upon a time, there were three little pigs. They all decided to go off on their own, because their parents decided they were old enough, and furthermore, they were getting on Papa Piggy's nerves. Off they went one bright sunny morning, but they suddenly realized they had no place to live. The first little pig, whose name was Harold, decided to build a house out of wood. He did a little figuring, got all his money together (which was $459.29), and went bounding off to the local building supply store. He got a large cart and picked up the items listed in the box below.

If he needed at least $45.00 for food, did he have enough money to build the house and buy food? If not, how much money did he need to make up the difference?

$12\frac{1}{5}$, one-by-six-inch boards	@ $12.95 ea.
$14\frac{2}{3}$, two-by-four-inch boards	@ $10.59 ea.
$5\frac{3}{4}$ boxes of three-penny nails	@ $3.95 ea.
$3\frac{1}{2}$ boxes of floor tile	@ $23.65 ea.
$2\frac{1}{2}$ gallons of paint	@ $12.50 ea.

Fraction Card Games

ASSIGNMENTS AND GUIDELINES:

This week, you will be working with a partner to design and create a card game involving fractions. The requirements are as follows:

1. Make a card game, similar to Concentration, War, or another game you know.
2. Include the following concepts within the game as creatively as you can:

   a. equivalent fractions: ex. $\frac{3}{4} = \frac{9}{12}$

   b. creating fractions with like denominators   ex. $\frac{3}{4}$ and $\frac{1}{2}$ = $\frac{3}{4}$ and $\frac{2}{4}$

   c. identifying proper and improper fractions and mixed numbers

   d. converting mixed numbers to improper fractions and vice versa

   e. simplifying fractions and improper fractions   ex. $\frac{8}{12} = \frac{2}{3}$ and $\frac{14}{8} = 1\frac{3}{4}$

   f. finding greatest common factors between two numbers
      ex. between 12 and 16, the greatest common factor is 4

   g. finding the least common multiple
      ex. between 15 and 9, the least common multiple is 45

3. Make a clear and specific set of directions. Your evaluation will be based on all of the above requirements.

A MATCHING CARD GAME LAYOUT

Name the fraction equivalent for 60%.	Name three equivalent fractions of $\frac{1}{4}$.	Name the simplified form of $\frac{16}{5}$.	30
$3\frac{1}{5}$	What is the greatest common factor of 27 and 18?	$\frac{15}{18}$ and $\frac{4}{18}$	$\frac{3}{5}$
What is the least common multiple between 15 and 6?	Name the fractions with the least common denominators for $\frac{5}{6}$ and $\frac{2}{9}$.	9	$\frac{3}{12}$ $\frac{6}{24}$ $\frac{5}{20}$

Fraction Puzzle Booklets

ASSIGNMENTS AND GUIDELINES:

This week, you will be working with a partner to make a puzzle booklet and an answer key. A puzzle booklet is made up of all kinds of games and questions. Perhaps you used to take these books on long trips when you were younger. After we complete our books, we will exchange them with another pair. Here are the guidelines:

1. Your booklet must include all kinds of fraction problems: addition, subtraction, multiplication, and division.
2. You should include a variety of concepts:
   a. equivalent fractions
   b. fractions of greater or lesser value
   c. simplifying fractions
   d. changing improper fractions to mixed numbers and vice versa
   e. least common multiple and greatest common factor
3. You may include a variety of activities such as: matching, word searches, crossword-puzzles, and "find the shape" searches. (ex. find the pieces that make up ...)
4. You may use a computer to make your book.

SAMPLE PUZZLE QUESTIONS:

Draw a line to match the following fractions with their equivalents:

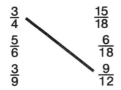

$$\frac{3}{4} \qquad \frac{15}{18}$$

$$\frac{5}{6} \qquad \frac{6}{18}$$

$$\frac{3}{9} \qquad \frac{9}{12}$$

If one of the pieces shown in the shape below is equal to $\frac{1}{4}$, color enough of the blocks blue to equal $3\frac{1}{2}$. Then color 50% of the whole shape red.

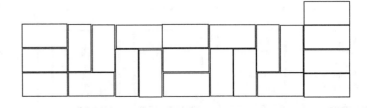

Geometric Rockets

ASSIGNMENTS AND GUIDELINES:

This week, you will draw and color a poster-sized rocket. Here is a list of your assignments for the week:

1. Use all the geometric shapes listed below to draw a rocket.
2. Make a small drawing, which must be done accurately on a piece of art paper measuring 9 inches by 12 inches. Draw the rocket using only a pencil, a ruler, a protractor, and a compass.
3. Use at least one of each shape that is listed; however, you may use many <u>more</u> of each.
4. Now, draw the rocket on the poster much bigger than you did on the small paper.
5. After you complete the big drawing, measure the lines from which your shapes are made. Record all the lengths, **right on the poster**.
6. Using the formulas for area below, find the total area of your rocket. You may have to divide some of the large shapes into smaller ones to find the area. Keep the answer on a separate piece of paper to use later.
7. Now, exchange rockets and find the total area of another person's rocket. When you find the area, return the rocket to its creator.
8. Check the answer on your rocket, color your rocket, and share it with the class.

USE THESE SHAPES TO MAKE THE ROCKET:

Shape: Area:

1. square.............. length x width

2. rectangle.......... length x width

3. triangle............. (base x height) ÷ 2

4. circle................ radius x radius x 3.14

5. parallelogram... divide the shape into two triangles and a rectangle, and then find the area of each shape

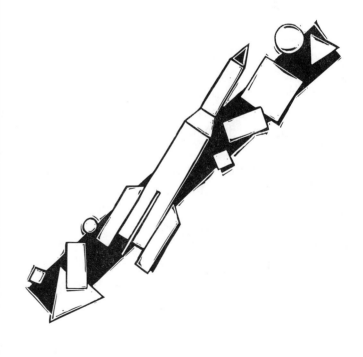

Geometry Zip-Around Game

ASSIGNMENTS AND GUIDELINES:

This week, you will be working with a partner to make a zip-around game using geometry terms. There are many categories of geometry, so your teacher will assign you a category. Then, follow these guidelines:

1. Using your textbook and any other references you have, look up the definitions of the terms in your category. On a piece of loose-leaf paper, write down 10 or 15 words and their definitions, like this:

    1. equilateral triangle - a three-sided figure with sides equal in length
    2. hexagon - a six-sided polygon
    3. scalene triangle - a triangle with no congruent sides

    (and so on in the same way)

2. Then, on 10 or 15 large index cards, in large print, copy the definition for the above number one, towards the bottom of card number one.

3. On the top of card number 2, write the name or word that answers the definition on card number one. If you study the game at the right, it will help you understand.

4. On the bottom of card number two, ask who has the definition for question number 2 ... and so on.

5. Remember, you should very carefully go in the order of the words and definitions you first wrote on loose-leaf paper at the beginning of this assignment.

6. Another thing to remember is that the last card you do has the last definition on your list, but you must put its matching word at the top of the very first card.

SAMPLE ZIP-AROUND CARDS:

1. I have a square...
   WHO has a three-sided figure with sides equal in length?

2. I have an equilateral triangle...
   WHO has a six-sided polygon?

3. I have a hexagon...
   WHO has a triangle with no congruent sides?

4. I have a scalene triangle...
   WHO has an exact location?

5. I have a point...
   WHO has a shape formed by 2 rays?

6. I have an angle...
   WHO has two lines that cross at 90° angles?

7. I have perpendicular lines...
   WHO has 2 angles whose sum = 180°?

8. I have supplementary angles...
   WHO has a 4-sided, 2-D figure with equal sides?

Geometry Dictionary

ASSIGNMENTS AND GUIDELINES:

This week, you will be writing a dictionary of geometric terms for younger children. Each term must be accompanied by an illustration. When you complete the book, perhaps you will have the opportunity to discuss it with a partner, a younger student, or a sibling. Here are the guidelines for the week:

1. Using your math book or a geometry book from the school library, make a list of geometry terms you would like to place in your dictionary. Be sure to explain each term in language that is easy to understand. Make a rough illustration of each term that you choose. You should have at least 20 terms in your dictionary.

2. Get some white or light-colored art paper, and fold it in half like a book.

3. Print the definitions very neatly in the booklet, or if computers are available, print out the definitions in a large font style, and glue them in the booklet.

4. Draw the illustration of each geometry term either beside the definition or beneath it.

5. Share your dictionary with a partner or a younger child.

SAMPLE DEFINITIONS AND LAYOUT:

1. CONE... **A shape that looks like an ice cream cone turned upside down. It has a circle for a base and a pointed tip.**

2. CUBE... **A shape that looks like a child's block. It has 6 sides, 8 corners, and 12 edges.**

3. ANGLE... **An open shape that is made of two lines called rays that touch at one end.**

4. CIRCLE... **A flat ball. If something is flat, we call it two-dimensional.**

5. SQUARE... **A flat, or two-dimensional, shape that has four sides that are all the same length. It has four right angles.**

"Guess and Check" Problems

ASSIGNMENTS AND GUIDELINES:

This week, you will be writing problems that require the "Guess-and-Check" strategy to solve. You have probably seen many of these problems in the past. An example is: I am thinking of two numbers. If I add them, I get a factor of 18, and if I subtract them, I get 3. What are the two numbers? To solve this problem, you "guess" any two numbers (probably below 10), and then "check" to see if the two numbers meet the requirements.

Many "guess-and-check" problems begin by saying: "I have some trucks ..." or "Tom, Jerry, and Sam had some candy ..." Then, they go on to say more specific amounts owned by each, but they always leave out one amount, which the problem-solver has to figure out. Your assignment this week is to write five or more of these problems. You may need to consult your textbook for some ideas. You will find sample problems in the box below.

On another sheet of paper, solve the five problems that you write and keep your answers in a safe place. When you have completed the assignment, exchange your problems with another person in the class, and they will solve them.

SAMPLE PROBLEMS:

1. José and Freddy had some baseball cards. José had 2 times the number Freddy had. Together, they had 180 cards. How many did each of them have?

2. Samuel and Jacob went to the movie. The total cost of the movie tickets was $11.00. Samuel's ticket cost $2.50 more than Jacob's (because he was older). How much did each ticket cost?

3. Of the 36 artists attending the convention, there were 3 times as many watercolorists as there were oil painters. How many of each were there?

4. Billy had some cars. He had 2 times as many red ones as blue ones and 3 times as many yellow ones as red ones. If he had 18 cars, how many of each did he have?

Investing

ASSIGNMENTS AND GUIDELINES:

This week, you will study the stock market. Pretend to be an investor. You may find you can get rich (even if it is only pretend!). You will be given an imaginary $5,000, dividing the money evenly to buy 5 to 10 stocks. The guidelines for the week are as follows:

1. Select 5 to 10 stocks from the stock market page of the newspaper. You may do this randomly, or you may study the stock market from a newspaper or the Internet, and then choose some that you think may be successful.
2. Search the Internet or newspaper daily to track the rise and fall of your stock values. Make a recording chart to track your stocks, and record their daily rise or fall carefully.
3. At the end of the week, graph the ups and downs of your investments and develop a presentation for the class, listing the advantages and/or disadvantages of investing in the stocks you have chosen.

THE NEXT STEP:

In addition to the stock study, please choose one of the topics below and prepare a presentation:

1. Look into other areas of investing other than stocks and bonds, like buying real estate properties or rental properties. Choose one of the methods, do some research about it, and then report your findings to the class.
2. Find out the safest ways to invest money, as well as some risky investment methods.
3. Call a stockbroker and make an appointment for a phone interview with her/him about her or his job. Prepare your questions carefully before your call.
4. Do some research about one, two, or all of the investment markets or vehicles listed below, and present your findings to the class. You may want to say which of these you plan to invest in someday, and why:

   a. Dow Jones Industrial Average
   b. NASDAQ
   c. U.S. Treasury Bonds
   d. Mutural Funds
   e. S&P 500
   f. IRAs
   g. Certificates of Deposit (CDs)

Lunch Bag Volume

ASSIGNMENTS AND GUIDELINES:

This week, you will gather as many different lunch bags as you can find, and then find the volume of each. Then do the following assignments with this information.

1. Graph the results of your lunch bag volume calculations using a bar graph. Be prepared to share this with the class.

2. Find the volume of the items on the right and make a graph of these findings.

3. Find out how many items these bags will hold. The items you can use in your lunch bags are listed on the right.

4. Finally, design a new lunch bag, one that may be better than those on the market.

5. Then, make a model of the bag, find the total volume, and present your idea and the graphs you made to the class. Be sure you choose only healthy foods for your new bag!

ITEMS YOU MAY PLACE IN THE BAGS:

Item	Volume
a sandwich with two regular slices of bread	
a regular-sized candy bar (i.e., Snickers™)	
a piece of round fruit (apple, orange, or peach)	
5 vegetable sticks, 8 cm long (celery or carrots)	
a stack of 6 crackers	
a small plastic container measuring 4" x 4" x 4"	
a rectangular-prism-shaped box of juice	

Making a Division Game

ASSIGNMENTS AND GUIDELINES:

This week, you will work in a small group to complete a board game using division of whole numbers and decimals. The secret to a good game is that all problems should be able to be done mentally or have multiple-choice answers written on the question cards. Your assignments are as follows:

1. Make a small board game. Begin by making a prototype (first draft) using thin paper. Then, play the game, make revisions, and remake the final board game on heavy paper stock.

2. The game must have at least 40 problems to solve. The types of problems you must include are listed in the box below.

3. During the time it takes you to make this game, you are not permitted to use a calculator.

4. The final game must contain three very clear parts:
   a. the colorful board,
   b. at least 40 question cards (you may have more than 40),
   c. a very clear and specific set of directions.

5. When you finish your game, play the game, and make last-minute changes.

6. When the class is finished, we will exchange our games.

TYPES OF PROBLEMS:

1. estimation problems, involving one- and two-digit divisors
2. simple, quick division problems with one- and two-digit divisors
3. simple story problems for which students must choose the correct number sentence that represents the problem
4. problems that have a decimal divided by a whole number
5. problems that have a whole number divided by a decimal
6. problems that have a decimal divided by a decimal
7. problems where you must round the final answer
8. problems where you must carry the quotient out to the hundredths place

Making a "Find the Shapes" House

ASSIGNMENTS AND GUIDELINES:

This week, you will be working alone on a house design.

1. Construct a front view of the house.

2. Make a first-draft picture of your house on a smaller piece of art paper. On this small drawing, you do not have to draw the shapes in the exact sizes, as suggested in the box below. Just make this drawing as a rough plan for the large final house drawing. As you do the design, also make an answer key so you won't forget where each shape is located. Keep the answer key in a safe place.

3. Transfer this drawing to a large poster or piece of art paper (at least 18″ by 28″), and draw the final house as perfectly as you can. The house will be a kind of "Find the Shapes" page like you may have done when you were younger.

4. Make sure you include several overlapping shapes in the drawing, because that will make the shapes harder to find and more fun for your partner. Include the shapes listed in the box in your final house. Be sure to make your house as large as possible so the shapes are clearly visible.

5. Draw the entire house using any geometric tool that will help you.

6. Color your house. Exchange the houses. "Find the Shapes" in someone else's house. When all houses are complete, return to their creators for correction.

SHAPES TO INCLUDE:

1. One each of the following polygons:
   a. square
   b. rhombus
   c. rectangle
   d. trapezoid
   e. parallelogram
   f. pentagon

2. A pair of similar geometric shapes of each of the following:
   a. square
   b. rectangle
   c. rhombus

3. At least four 90° angles

4. Two circles with a circumference of 9.42 cm

5. Two circles with an area of 12.56 sq. cm

6. One each of the following triangles:
   a. equilateral
   b. isosceles
   c. scalene
   d. right
   e. acute
   f. obtuse

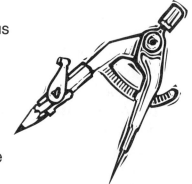

Making a Geometry Quiz

ASSIGNMENTS AND GUIDELINES:

This week, you will work with a partner to create a quiz for the students in your class. You will be assigned to a particular area of geometry and will develop your quiz on that material. Here is a list of your assignments for the week:

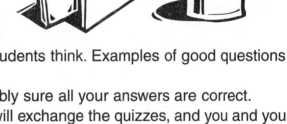

1. Create a 15-point quiz.
2. Base your questions on the area of geometry to which you have been assigned.
3. Make your questions open-ended, if possible. That means the questions must make the students think. Examples of good questions are given in the box below.
4. Make an answer key. Make doubly sure all your answers are correct.
5. On the due date, your teacher will exchange the quizzes, and you and your partner will do the quiz of another partnership while they do yours.
6. After all the quizzes are completed, return the quizzes to the partners for correction.

SAMPLE GEOMETRY QUIZ QUESTIONS:

1. Paolo wanted to build a wooden 5-sided box (no lid) that was 30 inches tall, 30 inches deep, and 30 inches wide. If the boards he wanted to use were 6 inches wide and 8 feet long, exactly how many boards would he need?

2. If our teacher wanted to make a curtain for a particular window in our classroom or hall, and he needed to double the width of the cloth to block out the light, how much material would he need if the fabric came in 54-inch widths?

3. How many square feet of carpeting would be needed to carpet this classroom?

4. One gallon of paint covers 225 square feet. How much paint would you need to paint five parking spaces, if each space measures 15 feet by 6 feet?

Making a Multiplication Activity Pamphlet

ASSIGNMENTS AND GUIDELINES:

This week, you will work with a partner to make a little activity booklet with an illustrated cover— something like the ones you take in a car on vacation. The final draft must be in black ink, fine-point black marker, or done on the computer. The problems or puzzles in your pamphlet must include the following types of multiplication of whole numbers, decimal numbers, or both:

1. Five problems that include estimating products.

2. Five problems that include drawing a picture to show the multiplication solution.

3. Five problems that include two-step problems.

4. Five problems that include three-step problems.

5. Five problems that demand the identification of a property of multiplication. The properties of multiplication are: the distributive property, the property of one, the commutative property, the associative property, and the zero property.

6. A separate and complete answer key that has been checked by both partners.

SAMPLE ACTIVITY BOOK PAGES:

ESTIMATION:
1. How many cows fell from the sky in a week, if 39 fell each day for 7 days? _____
2. How many beetles were shipped, if they packed them in 55 boxes? Each box had 18 beetles in each of 4 layers. _____

PROPERTIES OF MULTIPLICATION:
1. Which of these problems shows the distributive property of multiplication?
a. (456 x 578) + (23 + 65) =
b. 7 (3 + 6) = 21 + 42
c. 43 + 56 + 99 =
Explain your answer. _____
_____

TWO-STEP PROBLEMS:
1. There once was a girl from Rangoon, who often would belt out a tune. She sang 80 at noon on each day of June, and the rest of the year, she would croon two each day. How many tunes did she croon?_____

DRAW A PICTURE:
1. When Jon got treats for Halloween, he got 4 candy bars from 3 houses, 5 bite-sized candies from each of 4 houses, and 2 popcorn balls from 7 houses. He also got one piece of fruit from 34 houses and 7 packs of gum. How many treats in all?_____

Math Manipulatives Lesson

ASSIGNMENTS AND GUIDELINES:

This week, you will work with a small group to develop a lesson using math manipulatives that could be presented to younger children. You will present your lesson to your class and, if possible, to a younger class. To make it easier, use dried beans, color tiles, small blocks, or whatever is available. Follow these guidelines:

1. Develop an entire lesson on transparencies.

2. Introduce yourselves and write a very clear set of rules that will be presented to the younger children in the beginning of your lesson. For instance:
   a. Do not touch the bag of beans we give you until you are told to do so.
   b. If you drop a bean, please pick it up.
   c. If you have a question, please raise your hand—no talking out of turn.

3. Write the objective or goal that you have for the lesson, and go over it with the class.

4. Write two very simple problems (addition or subtraction) like those shown below. On the overhead projector, show the children how to set up the beans or manipulatives in order to solve the problems. This will be a demonstration, so the students will just observe.

5. Write two more problems and read each of them to the students. Ask them to take the manipulatives and try to solve the problem. At this point, all the members of your group should circulate the room to assist the students.

6. When you have completed the lesson, present it to your class and, if possible, a younger group of students.

SAMPLE PROBLEMS:

PROBLEM ON TRANSPARENCY

SET-UP OF PROBLEM USING BEANS

PROBLEM ONE

Tommy had 4 trucks. In 2 of the trucks he put 3 stones. In another truck, he put 5 stones, and in the last truck he put 2 stones. How many stones were in all the trucks?

THESE BOXES ARE THE TRUCKS:

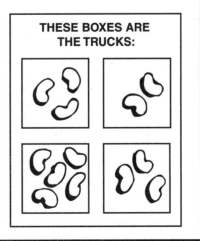

Pattern Story Problems

ASSIGNMENTS AND GUIDELINES:

This week, you will be writing story problems in which there is a pattern. For example: Once there was a girl who ate two apples on Monday, four apples on Tuesday, and six apples on Wednesday. If this pattern continues, how many apples did she eat on Saturday? In this problem, you have to set up a list or table to solve it. Here is one way to do this:

Mon.	Tues.	Wed.	Thurs.	Fri.	Sat.
2	4	6	8	10	12

Now that you have an idea of how to write this type of problem, write three story problems involving fractions, illustrate each, and make a table or list to help you solve each problem. Your teacher will give you two large pieces of paper. Write your three problems on this paper with the solutions as shown to the right. After you have completed this, you will share your problems with the class and ask the students how they would solve each problem.

SAMPLE PROBLEM:

Once upon a time, a little girl named Sarah owned 24 little toy cars. She decided to share them. She gave Billy $\frac{1}{6}$ of them, Sally $\frac{1}{2}$ of what she gave Billy, and Gerry $\frac{1}{2}$ of what she gave Sally. How many cars did she give away?

ILLUSTRATION:

PATTERN BOX:

Sarah	Billy	Sally	Gerry
24	4	2	1

Sarah started with 24 cars. She gave Billy $\frac{1}{6}$ of them, or 4 cars. Then she gave Sally $\frac{1}{2}$ of what she gave Billy, or 2 cars. Finally, she gave Gerry $\frac{1}{2}$ of what she gave Sally, which was 1 car. Add together, 4 + 2 + 1 = 7. Sally gave away 7 cars.

Percent of Commercial Time on TV

ASSIGNMENTS AND GUIDELINES:

This week, you will be working in a small group to accomplish several tasks. You will have the unpleasant task of watching some television this week. You will be timing the commercials at certain times during the day on a certain channel in your area. Follow these guidelines as you work:

1. Make a poster like the one below.
2. Assign each member of your group a different channel to watch for one-half hour in the morning, one-half hour in the early afternoon, one-half hour in the late afternoon, and one-half hour at 8 P.M.
3. To record the commercial time, you will need either a stopwatch or a second hand on a watch and a piece of loose-leaf paper to record the minutes.
4. After you record all the minutes and seconds of commercial time within the half hour, add them up. Make a fraction of the total commercial time over the total airtime of 30 minutes, and convert this to a percent.
5. Place your findings on the poster. Can you see any differences in the commercial time in the morning, afternoon, and evening? Are there differences between channels?
6. List ten more studies that could be done using commercials on TV. Share your chart and ideas with the class.

	early morning	early afternoon	late afternoon	evening 8 PM
Jim channel A				
Wong channel B				
Pedro channel C				
Laticia channel D				

Pictures Help Solve Problems

ASSIGNMENTS AND GUIDELINES:

This week, you will be writing problems and drawing pictures to solve them. Drawing a picture to visualize a problem really helps us solve it. The following is a list of your assignments for the next few days:

1. Write three story problems that involve something real you can count, like cookies, buttons, apples, strawberries, or pancakes. Your problems may include any operation of whole numbers, fractions, or decimals. (It is a good idea if these items are also easy to draw.)

2. Second, transfer your problems to three large sheets of paper that your teacher will give you. Remember to allow room for the picture at the bottom of the paper and use one sheet of paper for each problem.

3. Third, on a piece of loose-leaf paper, draw the solutions for all three problems.

4. On the assigned day, exchange the problems on the large paper (without solutions) with a partner, and he/she will solve them right on the large paper. When they finish drawing their solutions, check their answers against yours. If time permits, share one of your problems with the class.

SAMPLE PROBLEM:

One rainy day, little Sam left his toy cars outside, and they got rusty. Another day, Sam took 10 toy cars (twice as many as he left in the rain) down to the pond, to see if they could float ... and of course, they sank! On the day of the first big snow, Sam took 25 of his cars outside to play with on his snow castle. But he forgot to bring them in, and you guessed it, they were ruined! His mom was so angry that he had lost half of his cars that she took away the remaining cars. How many cars did Sam lose altogether, and how many would he have now, if he had all the cars he started with?

Planning a Garden

ASSIGNMENTS AND GUIDELINES:

This week, you will work with a group to make plans for a vegetable or flower garden or a small section of each. You may use garden catalogs or newspaper ads to find the items that you need:

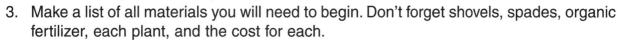

1. You have a budget of $300.00.

2. The area of the garden measures 20 feet wide by 20 feet long.

3. Make a list of all materials you will need to begin. Don't forget shovels, spades, organic fertilizer, each plant, and the cost for each.

4. Plan the garden on graph paper and then copy the plan to a transparency to share with the class.

5. If you choose to plant vegetables, make sure you provide enough space for them to grow. Some common vegetables and flowers are listed below, followed by the approximate area needed by each plant.

6. Be sure to provide areas in the garden as walkways to enable you to pick your flowers or vegetables.

7. Share the costs and the plan with the class.

PLANTS AND AREAS THEY NEED TO GROW

Vegetables:

1. tomatoes - 3 by 3 ft. & 8 ft. tall
2. green peppers - 2 by 2 ft. & 3 ft. tall
3. small hot chili peppers - 1.5 by 1.5 ft. & 2 ft. tall
4. lettuce, grown in rows, each row about 1 ft. wide
5. spinach, grown in rows, about 8 in. wide
6. cabbage - 2 by 2 ft. & 2 ft. tall
7. green onions, grown in rows, about 4 in. wide

Flowers:

1. sunflowers (from seed) about 1 ft. square, from 2 to 8 ft. tall
2. zinnias (from seed) about 6 in. square, from 2 to 5 ft. tall
3. bulbs: iris, tulip, daffodil, need 8 in. square, from 1 to 2 ft. tall
4. daisies (buy as a small plant), vary in area and height

Planning a School Supply Store

ASSIGNMENTS AND GUIDELINES:

This week, you will be working with a group of three or four students to plan an imaginary school supply store. The object of this shop is to raise money. The money will be used for a good cause, like to help the homeless or to enable the students in your school to go on a trip in their last year of school. The following lists your assignments for the week:

1. Decide where you will put the shop in your school; also why you are starting the shop.

2. Decide what you will sell in your shop. You will have to acquire catalogs to determine which items and for how much you will sell them in order to make an adequate profit.

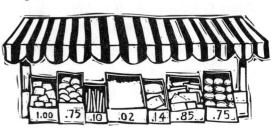

3. Decide who will run the shop (students, parents, or employees?).

4. Decide how much money you need to begin the shop.

5. Where will you get the money to buy your first products? Will you have an initial fund-raiser?

6. Will you have an adult sponsor? (This may be necessary from the school administration's point of view.)

7. Finally, place the following on a poster:
   a. the location of your store and how it will run;
   b. every item you will sell;
   c. how much each item costs and what you will sell it for; and
   d. the percent profit you will make on each item.

OTHER ITEMS TO CONSIDER:

1. Where will you order the school supply shop items? Who will give you the lowest price?

2. How will you decide what to sell the items for? Will you mark the items up by 50%, 75%, or 100%? Will students buy the items if they are outrageously expensive?

3. If you have students man the shop, when will they be able to do this? Will they miss their lunch period or use study hall time to work in the shop?

4. Who will calculate the earnings and do the buying for your shop?

5. Will you open a bank account? Which bank offers the highest interest so that your money will increase?

6. What will you do with your profits?

Planning a Vacation

ASSIGNMENTS AND GUIDELINES:

This week, you will be planning a pretend trip. You will work with a group of three or four other students to do this. It is a much more difficult task than you think to plan a vacation, but you will give it a whirl this week. The materials you will need are: maps of the United States (a United States atlas would be good), scratch paper, and a large piece of paper to do your final recordings. These are some rules you must follow:

1. Your trip will last exactly fourteen days—no more, no less.
2. You must drive a car, van, or cross-country vehicle (be careful about gasoline consumption).
3. You have exactly $4,000 to spend, and you must stay within this budget.
4. You are going as a group, but you must have an adult with you to drive, so choose one parent as driver/chaperone.
5. You may go anywhere in the mainland USA. Be sure to consider what the whole group would like to see and make some compromises so that each person gets to go to at least one place of his/her choice. Share the plans for your trip with the class.

THINGS TO CONSIDER:

1. Remember to calculate how many miles you can travel daily (use the distance scale). Then see if you can make it to all the spots you plan to visit. (You may have to make several adjustments.)
2. You should make a daily time schedule showing how much time you need to sleep, eat, sightsee, and relax each day. You will have to adjust this carefully, depending on where you will be each day.
3. Make a detailed list of the expenses, showing how much you will spend each day on gasoline (you will have to find out how many miles per gallon the car gets), on food, on motel rooms, and on all the other expenses. Do not forget to provide spending money to each person after you have made sure you can meet all other costs.

4. Remember to begin your trip in your town and move out from that spot to your destinations, one place at a time. Good luck!

Positive and Negative Numbers

ASSIGNMENTS AND GUIDELINES:

This week, you will be writing story problems involving positive and negative numbers. To do this, you must first understand the various rules for working with these numbers. Study the pages in the book that you are assigned, and try some operations with these numbers before you begin the project. The following lists your assignments for the next few days:

1. Write three story problems with solutions.
    a. In one of the problems, draw a picture to achieve the answer.
    b. In the second problem, make a table or list in order to come to the solution.
    c. The third will be one that you must work backwards to solve.

2. It may help to find a couple of examples of each of these problems and try them out as a review.

3. Finally, choose your best story problem and make a visual of the solution to share with the class. The visual may be a poster, a transparency, or a video.

SAMPLE PROBLEM:

Ivy placed $5,000.00 in the bank at the beginning of the year. The account earned 5% interest on the balance of the money remaining in the bank on the 7th of the month, once each month. On the 30th of January, she paid her bills, and they totalled $4,990.00. On the 31st of January, she received an unexpected bill for $550.00, which she then paid. Each time her account went into the "red," or the negative digits, she was charged $15.00. On February 1st, Ivy deposited $4,500.00, and then on February 26th, proceeded to pay out $3,200.00 in bills. On February 27th, she received another unexpected bill for $1,780.00. She immediately paid this bill, and on March 1st, she deposited $4,000.00 into the account. On March 26th, she paid out $4,100.00 in bills. Does she have a balance on March 30th, or a deficit? If so, how much?

Probability and Prediction

ASSIGNMENTS AND GUIDELINES:

This week, you will be learning about probability and how mathematicians use it to make predictions. A prediction is almost like a hypothesis in science. You will be designing a way to collect data and then using that collection to predict what will happen when you try to collect the data a second time. A few ideas are in the box below. The following is a list of your assignments:

1. Choose an item that you can toss or spin which will give you an outcome of some type. For example, you could choose a spinner from an old game, a coin that will give you either heads or tails, or a six-sided die.
2. Decide how you will collect your data and then make a chart on which to record the data. Begin collecting your data a set number of times; for instance, if you chose to toss a coin, you might toss it 100 times to begin.
3. Study the outcomes from your chart and make a prediction about what you think will happen when you toss the coin another 100 times.
4. Toss the coin an additional 100 times. Do you think you could make a more accurate prediction about what would happen if you tossed it 100 more times?

SUGGESTIONS FOR PROBABILITY PROJECTS:

1. When tossing a die, how many times does the 3 come up in 50 tosses?
2. When spinning a spinner, how many times out of 50 spins can you spin the highest number on the spin board?
3. When tossing two coins, how many times out of 50 do you get double heads?
4. What chance is there of throwing doubles of any number when throwing two dice 50 times?
5. If I have one red, one yellow, and one blue cube in a brown bag, how many times out of 50 will I pick the red cube out of the bag?
6. If I have three coins, what chance is there of tossing three heads or three tails out of 50 tosses?

Producing a Math Survey

ASSIGNMENTS AND GUIDELINES:

This week, you will work with a group to write and conduct a survey about math. This survey will be given to a total of three classes in your school, one class at one grade level, a second at another grade level, and so on. (However, if you can only question one grade level, it will work just as well.) Your assignments for the week are as follows:

1. Write five or ten questions about math that have only two possible answers.

2. Get the questions approved by the teacher.

3. Revise and edit the questions, and then type them as shown in the box below.

4. Copy the survey so that you have enough copies for the class(es) you will visit.

5. Make an appointment with each of the classroom teachers to come to their class for a ten- or fifteen-minute period of time to conduct the survey with their students.

6. Write a short speech to say to the class before the survey is distributed to them, telling why you are conducting this survey.

7. After your survey is complete, tally your results. Find the percentages of the students that chose one answer or the other. Decide on a way to display the results on a bar graph or circle graph.

8. When you have completed all the assignments, make a presentation about your results to your class.

SAMPLE QUESTIONS:

1. Would you consider math to be one of your favorite subjects?

   ☐ Yes, I would. ☐ No, I would not.

2. In the future, do you think you will use math more in your home or at your work?

   ☐ At home ☐ At work

3. It has been reported on the news that American students are not as good in math as many other students around the world. Do you think this is true?

   ☐ Yes, I do. ☐ No, I do not.

Ratios of Age to Height

ASSIGNMENTS AND GUIDELINES:

This week, you will be working with a partner to collect and graph data of children's heights and their ages. You will analyze the data you have collected to find the connection between age and height. Your assignments are as follows:

1. Choose two classrooms of different age groups in your school.

2. Write a letter to the teachers in the classes, asking permission to come to each class to measure each child and ask the ages of the children. The letter should include the following information:

   a. Tell the teacher that it should take about 30 minutes for you to get the information from the class.

   b. Ask the teacher to sign the letter if he/she agrees that you may come into the class.

   c. Give the teacher a choice of 30-minute time blocks when he/she will permit you to come in.

   c. Ask the teacher to include a class list so you can place the names on your chart.

   d. Ask that the teacher return the permission slip to your teacher or to you.

3. Make a chart recording the names of the children and a space to put the age and height of each child.

4. After collecting the data, graph the information you have obtained and share this with the class.

INCLUDE THE FOLLOWING IN YOUR PRESENTATION:

1. A graph showing the ages of the younger group
2. A graph showing the heights of the younger group
3. A graph showing the ages of the older group
4. A graph showing the heights of the older group
5. A graph showing the average ages and heights of the younger group and the older group
6. A transparency showing the ratio of age to height of the younger and older groups

Splendid Story Problems

ASSIGNMENTS AND GUIDELINES:

This week, you will be writing story problems. Each day you will write five good problems, following the guidelines below. You are to write a first draft and a final draft for each set of problems. The final draft may be printed or typed, depending on the directions given to you by the teacher.

DAY ONE: 1-STEP PROBLEMS

Write 5 one-step story problems. These are problems that involve only one operation. You may use any of the four operations: addition, subtraction, multiplication, or division of whole numbers, fractions, decimals, or percents. You may also use geometry. After you complete each problem, write the answer on the reverse side of the paper. Here are some examples:

1. Charlie went to buy a bag of candy. He got 20 grape-flavored lollipops, 15 gummy worms, 35 sweet tarts, and 47 chocolate bears. How many pieces of candy did he buy altogether?
2. Susie took four of her friends out to a health food store; they each got a frozen yogurt cone that cost $1.39 each. How much was Susie's bill?

DAY TWO: 2-STEP PROBLEMS

Write 5 two-step story problems. These are the types of problems that you must do two different operations to solve them . Here is an example of this type of problem:

1. Tom raced his three cows. Mabel ran the mile in 15.6 minutes. Carla ran it in 16.5 minutes. Wilma ran the mile in 35.8 minutes. What was the average time for the three cows?

First, you have to add the three numbers. Then, division is necessary to find the average. If you want to enrich your story problems, you could make them about funny things or things that could never occur. For example, you might write about fleas that go on a shopping spree or owls that punch a time card.

DAY THREE: MULTI-STEP PROBLEMS

Write 5 multi-step problems that require several operations. Try to be creative as you write today. Use descriptive language, colors, flavors, and unusual sights in your problems. Here is an example:

Muffy the mouse got a job as a visiting mouse nurse. Her salary was $350.00 a month. She needs you to calculate a reasonable budget for her. Will she have enough money left over to go to the movies twice a month? Each movie ticket costs $2.75.

mouse house rent.................31%
mouse phone.........................6%
mousemobile........................21%
mouse food..........................10%
utilities..................................8%
mouse wardrobe..................12%
uniforms, misc. 8%

Story Problems With Combinations

ASSIGNMENTS AND GUIDELINES:

This week, you will be working with a partner to study and write story problems that involve combinations. You have worked many problems like this before. Study the sample problem below and write five problems of a similar nature. Your assignments are as follows:

1. Write five problems this week. In your problems, you might include different flavors of ice cream and the combinations of ice cream you can get in a sundae or a cone. You may want to use five or six pizza toppings and see how many three-topping pizzas you can get out of these various toppings.

2. Edit your problems and either print them very neatly on transparencies or print them out on a computer and ask your teacher to make transparencies of the problems.

3. On a day your teacher chooses, he/she will either put the transparencies up on the screen and you will solve them as a group, or he/she will give them to you for warm-up problems at the beginning of class for several days.

4. As the students in the class complete your problems, they will return them to you for corrections.

SAMPLE PROBLEM:

Jeannie and Suzie were best friends, but they liked to be original. Unlike most friends, they had exactly the same outfits, but they never wore exactly the same thing. In fact, they wore entirely different, unmatching outfits each day. They each had the following items:

1. One red t-shirt
2. One yellow t-shirt
3. One blue t-shirt
4. One pink t-shirt
5. One pair of green shorts
6. One pair of black shorts
7. One white skort
8. One black skort

How many different outfits can each girl make with one top and one pair of shorts or a skort?

For example:

1. red tee + green shorts
2. red tee + black shorts, etc.

Titanic Brain Teasers

ASSIGNMENTS AND GUIDELINES:

This week, you will be working with a small group to develop a booklet of *Titanic* brain teasers about the ship of the same name. Use the facts provided or do your own research to find additional facts. You should make problems out of the facts. Examples of brain teasers are given below.

FACTS ABOUT THE RMS *TITANIC*:

1. Length: 882 feet, 8 inches (268 meters)
2. Weight: 24,900 tons empty, 46,328 tons loaded
3. Height: 60.5 feet up to the boat deck; 9 decks or floors
4. 159 furnaces, heating a total surface of 144,142 sq. ft.
5. Lifeboats: 14 measuring 30′ long by 9′1″ by 4′ deep, capacity: 65 persons
   2 measuring 25′2″ long by 7′2″ by 3′ deep, capacity: 40 persons
   4 collapsible 27′5″ long by 8′ by 3′ deep, capacity: 47 persons
6. Personal flotation devices: 3,560 and 49 life buoys
7. Fuel usage: 825 tons daily
8. Water consumption: 14,000 gallons fresh water daily
9. Top speed: 23 knots
10. Provisions:
    a. meat–75,000 lbs.
    b. fish–11,000 lbs.
    c. bacon & ham–7,500 lbs.
    d. eggs–40,000
    e. potatoes–40 tons
    f. lettuce–7,000 heads
    g. ice cream–1,750 lbs.
    h. coffee–2,200 lbs.
    i. rice & beans–10,000 lbs.
    j. tomatoes–3,500 lbs.
11. Passengers: 2,228 persons (including crew)
12. Survivors: 711 persons
    (Hint: Look up the *Titanic* on Internet sites to find out more exciting facts.)

SAMPLE BRAIN TEASER QUESTIONS:

1. How many passengers would have survived the sinking had all lifeboats been filled to capacity?
2. How many pounds of meat were planned for each passenger and crew member?
3. Could the lifeboats have been connected to provide more room for passengers? Make a drawing of your plan.
4. How many pounds of fuel were used for each pound of the loaded ship?
5. Traveling at 20.5 knots, how fast was the ship going in miles per hour?

Wallpapering vs. Painting a Room

ASSIGNMENTS AND GUIDELINES:

This week, you will use the room dimensions below to decide whether to wallpaper or paint the room. You will write all the information on poster or chart paper and present it to the class on the assigned day. Your goal is to find the most economical thing to do. You will work alone using the following information to solve the problem:

1. The wallpaper you will use measures 18 inches wide and costs $12.99 for a roll of 20 feet. You will also need a gallon of paste for the paper, which costs $23.00.

2. The paint you will use costs $15.99 a gallon, and it has a coverage of about 350 square feet. You will need to paint the room with 3 coats of paint. The painting tools you will need cost an additional $35.00 (brushes, rollers, edger, tape).

3. The wallpaper hanger charges $16.00 an hour and has given you the estimate that it will take him 20 hours to hang the paper.

4. The painter charges $12.00 an hour and has given you the estimate that it will take her 20 hours to paint the room.

5. Work up the total costs and be prepared to present your findings to the class.

ROOM DIMENSIONS:

1. There are four walls in the room; the shape of the room is basically a rectangular prism.

2. The room is 21 feet long, 15 feet wide, and 8 feet tall.

3. On the first, shorter wall, there is one doorway, measuring 30 inches wide and 80 inches high.

4. On the second wall, a longer wall, there is a window, measuring 70 inches wide and 55 inches high.

5. On the third, shorter wall, there is another window, measuring three feet wide and 54 inches high.

6. The fourth wall (a longer wall) has no window or door.

    Remember, you do not paint or wallpaper the ceiling.

"Who Am I?" Game

ASSIGNMENTS AND GUIDELINES:

This week, you will be working with a partner to make a geometry "Who Am I?" game. Here are the assignments:

1. You will be given a particular area of geometry that you must research.
2. From this, develop three, four, or five clues for each term you want the class to identify. (Examples are given below.)
3. You will have between 20 and 30 terms to identify for your game.
4. You will be given the largest size of index card. Print each set of clues on the card, 3 spaces tall, in marker (the whole class needs to be able to see the clues from any place in the classroom), or you may print them out on a computer (48-point font).
5. On the assigned day, be prepared to share your game.

"WHO AM I?" SAMPLE CLUES:

1. I am a quadrilateral.
2. I have 2 sets of parallel sides.
3. I have no right angles.
4. I have 4 sides of equal length.
   WHO AM I? answer: a rhombus

1. I am a figure in space.
2. I have 4 corners.
3. I have no right angles.
4. I have 4 faces.
5. I have a triangular base.
   WHO AM I? answer: triangular
   pyramid

"Work-Backwards" Problems

ASSIGNMENTS AND GUIDELINES:

This week, you will be developing "work-backwards" story problems in math. These kinds of problems give the most important information last, and then you have to "work backwards" through the problem to find the solution. Your assignments for the week are as follows:

1. Write five "work-backwards" problems in rough-draft form.

2. Work the problems to find a solution for each.

3. Write the problems out on poster board or large chart paper. Use both sides of the paper and do not include the solution.

4. Choose the best problem you have written; get a partner to help you. Prepare a skit to act out the problem.

5. On the assigned day, present the skit to the class and see if anyone can solve the probelm. Explain how the problem was solved.

6. Exchange posters and see if another student in the class can solve the four additional problems you wrote. Or your teacher may choose to put one problem on the board each day for warm-up before class begins.

SAMPLE PROBLEMS:

1. Sara went to the mall. She spent $2.00 at the pharmacy, $4.00 for a pair of flip-flops, and then she went to lunch and spent $5.90. She had $3.10 remaining. How much money did she have to begin her shopping trip?

2. Paul baked cookies for "Cookie Day" at school. He gave 36 cookies to the cheerleaders and 59 cookies to the cooking class. He gave half of what he gave to the cheerleaders to the team mascot, and one-fourth of what he gave the cheerleaders to his best friend. His dog ate one-half of what he brought to school before he left home. How many cookies did he bake?

Writing About Long Journeys

ASSIGNMENTS AND GUIDELINES:

This week, you will be working with a group to develop mathematical story problems involving the trips of the great explorers, such as Magellan and Vasco da Gama. Type these story problems on the computer, if possible, or print them in black marker to enable the teacher to copy them for the class.

1. List some numerical facts you find about the various great explorers, for example, when they were born, when they died, how long their voyage(s) took, how far they traveled.

2. Write at least four story problems. Try to have some of your problems involve multi-plication of decimals.

3. Make your problems multi-step problems that involve more than one operation. Place only one or two problems on each page. ***Extra credit will be given if your problem involves a map, has a map key, or includes a chart or graph.**

4. Copy your problems in pen or type them on a computer. Be sure to leave room for the students to calculate a solution.

5. Turn in your first and second drafts of problems and a separate sheet with a detailed solution to each problem.

FACTS TO INSPIRE YOU:

1. A land mile is 5,280 feet; however, on water, a nautical mile is 6,080 feet.
2. In the 1600s, a large sailing vessel could achieve a daytime average of 1.7 nautical miles per hour. At night, because the winds usually decreased, they achieved a speed of less than that.
3. The *Mayflower* had a cargo of more than 360,000 pounds.
4. Barrels, which were used to store food, water, and grain, were stored side by side in the hold. Then it was found that more could fit in the hold if they were first placed down on their sides, then piled on top of each other.
5. Columbus left Spain on August 3, 1492, and arrived at San Salvador on October 12, 1492.
6. It is thought that Columbus's ship was 90 feet long and had 3 masts.